GANDHIAN SPIRITUALISM

GANDHIAN STUDIES AND PEACE RESEARCH SERIES

No. 1: **Gandhian Model of Development and world Peace**
R.P. Misra (Ed.)

No. 2: **Conflict Resolution Through Non-Violence: Role of the Universities — Volume I: Science and Ethics**
K.D. Gangrade and R.P. Misra (Ed.)

No. 3: **Conflict Resolution Through Non-Violence: role of Universities — Volume II: Development without Destruction**
K.D. Gangrade and R.P. Misra

No. 4: **The Social Philosophy of Mahatma Gandhi**
K.S. Bharathi

No. 5: **Gandhian Humanism**
Mohit Chakrabarti

No. 6: **Gandhian Holistic Economics**
Shashi Prabha Sharma

No. 7: **Gandhian Spiritualism: A Quest for the Essence of Excellence**

ABOUT THE AUTHOR

Mohit Chakrabarti (*b.* 1941) teaches Education and English at Visva Bharati University, Santiniketan 731235, India. Frequently participates and presents papers in National/International Conferences, Seminars, Symposia, Workshops etc. Significant participation/presentation/acceptance of papers in the World Assembly of Teacher-Educators at the University of the West Indies, Kingston, Jamaica, 1986; Beijing Normal University, Beijing, People's Republic of China, 1989; The Institute of Education, Republic of Singapore, 1990.

A translator, book-reviewer, poet and critic, profusely writes in many periodicals and research journals of repute in India and abroad.

A writer of children's books in English and Bengali, credited with more than two hundred papers, articles and creative writings.

Honoured with NATIONAL AWARD as a teacher-educator. A devoted, prolific and consistent contributor to studies in Rabindranath Tagore's educational thoughts and experiments and Gandhian philosophy and education.

Gandhian Studies and Peace Research Series 7

GANDHIAN SPIRITUALISM

A Quest for the Essence of Excellence

MOHIT CHAKRABARTI

Reader in Education
Visva Bharati University
Santiniketan

CONCEPT PUBLISHING COMPANY, NEW DELHI 110059

ISBN 81-7022-457-8

First Published 1993

Published and Printed by
Ashok Kumar Mittal
Concept Publishing Company
A/15-16, Commercial Block, Mohan Garden
NEW DELHI-110059 (India)

Lasertypeset by
Microtech Advance Printing Systems (Pvt.) Ltd.
H-13, Bali Nagar
NEW DELHI-110015

Dedicated to

SWAMI RANGANATHANANDA

who has been associated with the International Spiritual and Cultural Movement since 1926 and at whose feet I am fortunate to sit

BIBLIOGRAPHY

Aurobindo, Sri : *The Ideal of Human Unity*, Sri Aurobindo Pathamandir, Calcutta, 1972.

——— : *The Human Cycle*, Sri Aurobindo Pathamandir, Calcutta, 1972.

——— : *The Life Divine*, Sri Aurobindo Ashram, Pondicherry.

Bhattacharya, Buddhadeva : *Evolution of the Political Philosophy of Gandhi*, Calcutta Book House, Calcutta, [illegible].

Chakrabarti, Mohit : *Gandhian Mysticism*, Atlantic Publishers & Distributors, New Delhi, 1989.

——— : *The Gandhian Dimensions of Education*, Daya Publishing House, Delhi, 1990.

——— : *Gandhian* [illegible], Atlantic Publishers & Distributors, New Delhi, 1990.

——— : *Gandhian Humanism*, Concept Publishing Company, New Delhi, 1992.

Desai, Valji Govindji (Ed.) : *The Diary of Mahadev Desai*, Navajivan Publishing House, Ahmedabad, 1953.

Diwakar, R.R. : *Gandhi, the Spiritual Seeker*, Bharatiya Vidya Bhavan, Bombay.

Gandhi, M.K. : *An Autobiography*.

——— : *Hind Swaraj or Indian Home Rule*.

——— : *From Yeravda Mandir*.

——— : *Harijan*.

——— : *Young India*.

——— : *In Search of the Supreme*.

——— : *Speeches and Writings of Mahatma Gandhi*.

Mahadevan, T.K. (Ed.) : *Truth and Non-violence*, Gandhi Peace Foundation, New Delhi, 1970.

Nehru, Jawaharlal : *Mahatma Gandhi*, Asia Publishing House, Bombay, 1949.

Prabhu, R.K. & Rao, U.R. (Compiled) : *The Mind of Mahatma Gandhi*, Oxford University Press, London, 1945.

Pyarelal : *Mahatma Gandhi : The Last Phase*, Navajivan Publishing House, Ahmedabad, 1958.

PREFACE

To enter into the heartland of humanity is to search for the essence of excellence. Mahatma Gandhi, an apostle of inner excellence, invigorates humanity with the unending quest for the ascent that truly represents man as a spiritual aspirant. For such an ascent, Gandhi makes a practical approach to the day to day affairs of life from where man paves newer avenues for worthier excellence in spiritual poignance. "The Ascent of Man and Spiritualism: Gandhian Perspectives" is a quest for this end in view.

"Spiritual Education: Gandhian Viewpoints" spells out the manifold objectives of education as a spiritual experiençe, which even now awaits serious rethinking in the context of unfortunate ukase in education.

Spiritualism as a great exposure of the awakening of mass consciousness is yet to receive wider appeal. Admittedly, Gandhi launches his movement of *sarvodaya* not merely as an ethical and moral force, but essentially as an all-embracing spiritual revelation of humanity in course of synchronization of diverse behavioural designs. "*Sarvodaya* and Spiritualism: Gandhian Exposures" is an indepth analysis to negotiate this objective.

"The Aesthetics of Gandhian Spiritualism" is a critical approach to the intrinsic components of Gandhian aesthetics in relation to revelation of spiritual excellence, and, as such, it marks a significant avenue of spiritualism as a symbol of Truth, Goodness and Beauty.

That religion and spiritualism are closely interlinked, is an age-old truism that Gandhi emphasizes from the practical points of view. Man, in his spiritual vision, finds a newer approach to spiritualism only because he is primarily a harmonized being always striving for the good of one and all. "Religion and Spiritualism: The Gandhian Bonds of Harmony" is a critical study on this objective.

A mystic visionary *par excellence*, Gandhi wants humanity to be purified in best ideas, best thoughts and best sensibilities. As a source of his mystic force, the *Gita* plays the most significant role in harmonizing humanism and spiritualism. What he poignantly feels as a spiritual apostle is that the river of spiritual profoundness in man passes unnoticed and the flowers of mystic fragrance wither *sans* endearment *sans* adoration. In fact, he harps on love with a mystic detachment to bring forth the essence of the beyonding of man. Added to this are the mystic components of Truth and Tolerance which silently bring about a spiritual revolution in man. 'A reformer with a revolutionary', as Rabindranath Tagore succinctly appreciates, Gandhi repudiates toying with transitory happiness like 'spiritual atheletes' and emphasizes on delving deep into the mystic dimensions of spiritualism.

"Gandhian Spiritualism and the Modern World" is a synoptic study on the relevance of Gandhian spiritualism in negotiating global unrest in the most practical manner.

A comparative study of Mahatma Gandhi and Swami Vivekananda as spiritual apostles in "Gandhi and Vivekananda: Connoisseurs of Spiritual Consciousness" might add newer dimensions to the study on spiritualism and evoke a thrilling urge for the rediscovery of man as an unending spiritual force amongst revered readers and scholars.

I cannot but recall all the time the serene blessings of Revered Swami Ranganathanandaji Maharaj, President, Ramakrishna Math, Hyderabad-500029, to whom I humbly dedicate this book.

If spiritualism is adored and endeared from the Gandhian points of view, the world cannot but really be serene and new.

May I not ask myself aside for my research: Why not await the respected readers' profound and ardent comments?

Seemantika MOHIT CHAKRABARTI
Seemanto Palli
Visva Bharati University
Santiniketan 731 235

CONTENTS

Preface 7

1. The Ascent of Man and Spiritualism: Gandhian Perspectives 11
2. Spiritual Education: Gandhian Viewpoints 26
3. *Sarvodaya* and Spiritualism: Gandhian Exposures 57
4. The Aesthetics of Gandhian Spiritualism 80
5. Religion and Spiritualism: The Gandhian Bonds of Harmony 95
6. Gandhian Spiritualism: The Mystic Dimensions 112
7. Gandhi and Vivekananda: Connoisseurs of Spiritual Consciousness 130
8. Gandhian Spiritualism and the Modern World 169
9. Epilogue 177

Bibliography 180
Index 182

1

THE ASCENT OF MAN AND SPIRITUALISM: Gandhian Perspectives

Man alone craves for excellence eternal. He alone suffers from inadequacies and incompleteness internally and externally for he alone finds limitations of his endeavour to delve deep into the core of excellence, the starting point of his ascent as MAN. The mushrooms of inconsistencies diverse and manifold drive him to know himself, to have a complete control over himself and to be really worthy of himself. The beckonings of good sense and sensibilities in him are the buds of efflorescence that accelerate his ascent. The inherent sparkplugs of consciousness safeguard his spiritual sensibilities. He declares: *c'est moi* – Here I am. The signals of self-discipline and self-purification in him mark a new avenue of spiritualism as holistic components. Man born is reborn. The pale cast of ignorance is gradually removed. Man makes up to discover himself anew.

A spiritual apostle of ardent sensibilities, Gandhi probes into spiritualism in terms of harmony – physical, intellectual, social and cultural. He wants humanity to be crystallized in the service above self that brings the All Beautiful nearer to mankind. A mind thus controlled disallows all inconsistencies and delusions. It endears the endeavours of excellence because it is dynamic. And to be dynamic is to be in line with the ascent within. Such type of the ascent of man disapproves drab craze for utilitarianism that serves as a constraint to spiritualism. Gandhi's own exposition clarifies the point:

> A certain degree of physical harmony and comfort is necessary, but above that level, it becomes a hindrance instead of a help. Therefore the ideal of creating an unlimited number of wants and satisfying them seems to be a delusion and a snare. The satisfac-

> tion of one's physical needs, even the intellectual needs of one's narrow self must meet at a point a dead stop before it degenerates into physical and intellectual voluptuousness. A man must arrange his physical and cultural circumstances so that they may not hinder him in his service of humanity, on which all his energies should be concentrated.
>
> — M.K. Gandhi: *Harijan*, August 29, 1936, p. 226

To exceed human limitations either in the sphere of intellect or in that of physical needs is what Gandhi considers to be the most essential precondition for spiritualism. He thinks so because spiritualism evolves out of a purified and serene state of mind that makes a harmonious balance between the inherent needs of an individual and all other attractions in diverse dimensions. As a matter of fact, an individual exceeds himself when he thinks beyond himself and acts accordingly, and when he exceeds himself and thinks and acts so, he ascends the peak of spiritualism. This ascent is the birth of true humanity, which as Gandhi believes and actualizes in his life is true spiritualism. Such an ascent necessitates a long, continual, sustained and persuasive endeavour to conquer the little self and provide the human mind with ample opportunities to know the higher self, the Supreme Self which is in terms of spiritualism stands for the real *atman*. The greater the striving for the Supreme Self the better is the avenue of ascent for spiritualism. Even in political self-government as Gandhi firmly asserts, individual self-government plays a vital role and the latter, it is undeniable, greatly demands an individual's earnest endeavour for spiritual excellence. How does Gandhi himself make such an endeavour for continual inner excellence? What prompts him to advance for spiritual ascent? The practice of nonviolence that he sticks to is based upon the sound inner practice for self-purification in the form of self-restraint that allows ascent in spiritual excellence. For this, he makes his own platform — *Young India* that caters to continual self-refinement. His own exposition in this connection deserves attention :

> I have taken up journalism not for its sake but merely as an aid to what I have conceived to be my mission in life. My mission is to teach by example and precept under severe restraint the use of the matchless weapon of *Satyagraha* which is a direct corollary of

> non-violence and truth. I am anxious, indeed I am impatient, to demonstrate that there is no remedy for the many ills of life save that of non-violence. It is a solvent strong enough to melt the stoniest heart. To be true to my faith, therefore, I may not write in anger or malice. I may not write idly. I may not write merely to excite passion. The reader can have no idea of the restraint I have to exercise from week to week in the choice of topics and my vocabulary. It is a training for me. It enables me to peep into myself and to make discoveries of my weaknesses. Often my vanity dictates a smart expression or my anger a harsh adjective. It is a terrible ordeal but a fine exercise to remove these weeds. The reader sees the pages of the *Young India* fairly well-dressed-up and sometimes, with Romain Rolland, he is inclined to say 'what a fine old man this must be!' Well, let the world understand that the fineness is carefully and prayerfully cultivated. And, if it has proved acceptable to some whose opinion I cherish, let the reader understand that when that fineness has become perfectly natural, i.e., when I have become incapable of evil and when nothing harsh or haughty occupies, to it momentarily, my thought-world, then and not till then, my non-violence will move all the hearts of all the world. I have placed before me and my reader no impossible ideal or ordeal. It is man's prerogative and birth-right. We have lost the paradise only to regain it.
>
> — R.K. Prabhu and U.R. Rao (Compiled) : *The Mind of Mahatma Gandhi*, Oxford University Press, London, 1945, p.44

The ascent of the inner spirit for which Gandhi continually aspires is what serves as the essence of Gandhian spiritualism. Here is a continual aspirant for enlightenment of the inner self, — the sacred and serene self — who pays earnest endeavour to move all the world with his theory and practice or non-violence to be aware of utilizing and ennobling the qualities of the head and the heart that stand for spiritualism *par excellence*. For this, he emphasizes on elimination of animality that nurses bare passion and crushes the essentials of moral restraint. And when, as Gandhi categorically states, moral restraint is at stake, spiritualism badly suffers from the wounds of absence of awareness :

> It is wrong and immoral to seek to escape the consequences of

one's acts. It is good for a person who over-eats to have an ache and a fast. It is bad for him to indulge in his appetite and then escape the consequences by taking tonics or other medicine. It is still worse for a person to indulge in his animal passions and escape the consequences of his acts. Nature is relentless and will have full revenge for any such violation of her laws. Moral results can only be produced by moral restraints. All other restraints defeat the purpose for which they are intended.

Ibid., p. 108

How does self-restraint work as the highest source of inspiration for the ascent of man and for that end in view, of spiritualism? How is man better purified in his principles and actions through observance and maintenance of self-control that activates self-discipline and accelerates the true components of spiritualism? Gandhi elucidates the role of an individual from the standpoint of his own strivings for spiritual perfection by means of non-cooperation and non-violence that ultimately bring forth the spiritual emergence of freedom. As he observes,

There is no defence for my conduct weighed only in the scales of *ahimsa*, I draw no distinction between those who wield the weapons of destruction and those who do Red Cross work. Both participate in war and advance its cause. Both are guilty of the crime of war. But even after introspection during all these years, I feel that in the circumstances in which I found myself I was bound to adopt the course I did both during the Boer War and the Great European War and for that matter the so-called Zulu 'Rebellion' of Natal in 1906.

Life is governed by a multitude of forces. It would be smooth sailing, if one could determine the course of one's actions only by one general principle whose application at a given moment was too obvious to need even a moment's reflection. But I cannot recall a single act which could be so easily determined.

Being a confirmed war resister I have never given myself training in the act of destructive weapons in spite of opportunities to take such training. It was perhaps thus that I escaped direct destruction of human life. But so long as I lived under a system of government based an force and voluntarily partook of the many

> facilities and privileges it creates for me, I was bound to help that Government to the extent of my ability when it was engaged in a war unless I can cooperate with that government and renounced to the utmost of my capacity the privilege it offered me.
>
> — M.K. Gandhi : *Young India*, September 13, 1928

Explaining further the spiritual aspect of *ahimsa* in a letter addressed to H.S. Polak, Gandhi highlights the spiritual lesson for the people mesmerized in political turmoil, to be imparted in religious earnestness :

> What do you say to my recruiting campaign? It is for me a religious activity undertaken for the sacred doctrine of *ahimsa*, I have made the discovery that India has lost the power to fight — not the inclination. She must regain the power and then, if she will, deliver to a groaning world the doctrine of *ahimsa*. She must give abundantly out of her strength, not out of the weakness. She may never do it. That to me would mean her effacement. She would lose her individuality and would be like the other nations — a worshipper of brute force. This recruiting work is perhaps the hardest task yet undertaken by me. I may fail to gain recruits. I shall still have given the best political education to the people.
>
> — Quoted in Chandrasekhar Shukla (edited) : *Incidents of Gandhiji's Life*, Bombay, 1949, p. 245

The 'political education' that Gandhi refers to as above is in fact, the education for spiritual and moral enrichment and that type of education can only be achieved most solemnly by means of practice of performance in the inherent spirit of non-violence. How does non-violence work? Here is Gandhi's own opinion :

> Non-violence works in a most mysterious manner. Often a man's actions defy analysis in terms of non-violence; equally often his actions may wear the appearance of violence when he is absolutely non-violent in the highest sense of the term and is subsequently found as to be. All I can then claim for my conduct is that it was actuated in the interests of non-violence. There was no thought of sordid national or any other interest at the sacrifice of

some other interest.

I may not carry my argument any further. Language at best is but a poor vehicle for expressing one's thoughts in full. For me non-violence is not a mere philosophical principle. It is the rule and breath of my life. I know I fail often, sometimes consciously, more often unconsciously. It is a matter not of the intellect but of the heart. True guidance comes by constant waiting upon God, by utmost humanity, self-abnegation, by being ever ready to sacrifice one's self. Its practice requires fearlessness and courage of the highest order. I am painfully aware of my failings.

But the light within me is steady and clear. There is no escape for any of us save through truth and non-violence. I know that war is wrong, is an unmitigated evil. I know too that it has got to go. I firmly believe that freedom won through bloodshed or fraud is no freedom. Would that I shall still have given the best political education to the people.

Ibid.

The political education as referred to by Gandhi has a firmer identity in spiritualism that provides every person with an abundant inner force to combat against all evil and untoward forces. And when he thinks about a new brand of recruits in the operational arena of non-violence he strongly advocates such type of spiritual development as would gear up the entire humanity towards self-purification and self-enrichment.

How to gear up the global mankind for dissemination of such type of spiritualism? What are the essential components of spiritual enrichment? For Gandhi, mankind must seek spiritual poignance through exercise of the spirit of tolerance — a term very often misunderstood and misinterpreted as a mere tool of passive defence and rarely looked upon and exercised in terms of inner spiritual excellence. The efflorescence of Truth, Love and Beauty in man, as Gandhi ardently believes, primarily rests on the exercise of the spirit of tolerance from this end in view. His own exposure on this point is a clear revelation of the role of tolerance as the essence of spiritualism:

Tolerance may imply a gratuitous assumption of the inferiority of other faiths to one's own, whereas *ahimsa* teaches us to entertain the same respect for the religious faiths of others as we accord to

> our own, thus admitting the imperfection of the latter. This admission will be readily made by a seeker of Truth, who follows the law of Love. If we had attained the full vision of Truth, we would no longer be mere seekers, but have become one with God, for Truth is God. But being only seekers, we persecute our quest, and are conscious of our imperfection. And if we are imperfect ourselves, religion as conceived by us must also be imperfect. We have not realised religion in its perfection, even as we have not realised God. Religion of our conception, being thus imperfect, is always subject to a process of evolution and reinterpretation. Progress towards Truth, towards God, is possible only because of such evolution. And if all faiths outlined by men are imperfect, the question of comparative merit does not arise. All faiths constitute a revelation of Truth, but all are imperfect, and liable to error. Reverence for other faiths need not blind us to their faults. We must be keenly alive to the defects of our own faith also, yet not leave it on that account, but try to overcome these defects. Looking at all religious with an equal eye, we would not only not hesitate, but would think it our duty, to blend into our faith every acceptable feature of other faiths.
>
> — M.K. Gandhi : *From Yeravda Mandir*, Navajivan Press, Ahmedabad, 1935, p. 55

Crystallizing every religious faith by means of an ardent devotion to the essence of spiritualism is the fundamental point of departure in Gandhian spiritualism. It is that type of spiritualism which allows priority of the heart to the head, the inner beauty of religion to mere observance of rites and rituals. And what does tolerance actually do? Its real role is to eliminate the sense of autocracy and narrowness exposed in irreligious sentimentalism. When tolerance serves as a genuine component of spiritualism, it accelerates our insight to be hallowed with the true spirit of religion. As Gandhi explains by means of a simile :

> Even as a tree has a single trunk, but many branches and leaves, so there is one true and perfect Religion, but it becomes many, as it passes through the human medium, the one Religion is beyond all speech. Imperfect men put it into such language as they can command, and their words are interpreted by other men equally

> imperfect. Whose interpretation is to be held to be the right one? Everybody is right from his own standpoint, but it is not possible that everybody is wrong. Hence the necessity of tolerance, which does not mean indifference to one's own faith, but a more intelligent and purer love for it. Tolerance gives us spiritual insight, which is as far from fanaticism as the north pole from the south. True knowledge of religion breaks down the barriers between faith and faith.
>
> M.K. Gandhi, *From Yeravda Mandir, op. cit.*

The true essence of spiritualism is, therefore, the true ascent of man. It is this ascent in him that never allows intolerance either in the form of indifference or in that of hatred. As a consequence, the spirit of tolerance in every human being finds a new, strong, evolving, heightening spirit of fusion that steadily brings about a harmony of human consciousness. From the practical points of view, Gandhi illustrates by referring to the study of other religions that serve as a very favourable and effective strategy for exercising inner consciousness :

> One should study them (other religions) only through the writings of known votaries of the respective religions. For instance, if one wants to study the *Bhagavata*, one should do so not through a translation of it made by a hostile critic but one prepared by a lover of the *Bhagavata*. Similarly, to study the *Bible* one should study it through the commentaries of devoted Christians. This study of other religions besides one's own will give one a grasp of the rock-bottom unity of all religions and afford a glimpse also of the universal and absolute truth which lies beyond the 'dust of creeds and faiths'.
>
> Let no one even for a moment entertain the fear that a reverent study of other religions is likely to weaken or shake one's faith in one's own. The Hindu system of philosophy regards all religions as containing the elements of truth in them and enjoins an attitude of respect and reverence towards them all. This of course, presupposes regard for one's own religion, study and appreciation of other religions need not cause a weakening of that regard; it should mean extension of that regard to other religions.
>
> — M.K. Gandhi : *Young India*, December 6, 1928

That a man heightens his religious sensibilities by means of broadening the canvas of universal acceptability of the march of man towards nobler and finer visions of spiritualism is the most fundamental contribution to the development of spiritualism. And for this Gandhi considers the worth of man to be ascertained and evaluated in terms of ceaseless endeavour towards greater evolution. He has a unique pattern for ascending the steps of spiritual consciousness through service towards community not for bare exhibitionism but essentially for self-realization that as already referred to, serves as a major component of spiritualism. As he observes:

> If I found myself entirely absorbed in the service of the community, the reason behind it was my desire for self-realization. I had made the religion of service my own, as I felt that God could be realized only through service. And service for me was the service of India, because it came to me without my seeking, because I had an aptitude for it. I had gone to South Africa for travel, for finding an escape from Kathiawad intrigue and for gaining my own livelihood. But as I have said, I found myself in search of God and striving for self-realization.
>
> — M.K. Gandhi : *An Autobiography, op. cit.,* p. 97

With self-restraint as the component of spiritual ascent and excellence, Gandhi believes that a proper synchronization of body and mind in thought, word and deed should welcome *brahmacharya*. This is, in fact, an opener of the doors and avenues of true spiritualism. Whatever strategies are applied for this purpose in fasting and dieting are nothing but gradual preparations for reaching excellence of spiritual endeavour. Gandhi's own viewpoints explicitly unfold the objectives :

> I was anxious to observe *brahmacharya* in thought, word and deed, and equally anxious to devote the maximum of time to the *Satyagraha* struggle and fit myself for it by cultivating purity. I was therefore led to make further changes and to impose greater restraints upon myself in the matter of food. The motive for the previous changes had been largely hygienic, but the new experiments were made from a religious standpoint.
>
> Fasting and restriction in diet now played a more important part

> in my life. Passion in man is generally coexistent with a hankering after the pleasures of the palate. And so it was with me. I have even encountered many difficulties in trying to control passion as well as taste, and I cannot claim even now to have brought from them under complete subjection. I have considered myself to be a heavy eater. What friends have thought to be my restraint has never appeared to me in that light. If I had failed to develop restraint to the extent that I have, I should have described lower than the beasts and met my doom long ago. However, as I had adequately realised my short-comings, I made great efforts to get rid of them, and thanks to this endeavour I have all these years pulled on with my body and put in with it my share of work.
>
> — M.K. Gandhi : *An Autobiography, op. cit.*, p. 991

Looking after the essence of spiritualism through observance of fasting and control of passions as practised by Gandhi, makes a new departure in spiritual endeavour. That purity of thought and action, passion and contemplation, self-restraint and devotion goes a long way in the ascent of man as a spiritual being is an altogether new lesson to be learnt from Gandhian spiritualism. As a matter of fact, Gandhi further spells out the objective of fasting in relation to self-restraint as follows :

> Fasting can help to curb animal passion, only if it is undertaken with a view to self-restraint. Some of my friends have actually found their animal passion and palate stimulated as an after-effect of fasts. That is to say, fasting is futile unless it is as accompanied by an incessant longing for self-restraint.
>
> — *Ibid.*, p. 406

Moreover,

> Fasting and similar discipline is, therefore, one of the means to the end of self-restraint, but if it is not accompanied by mental fasting, it is bound to end in hypocrisy and disaster.
>
> — *Ibid.*

As a practical initiator in the practice of the essence of spiritualism,

Gandhi gives greater importance to self-restraint. The role of the teacher advocating spiritualism cannot but sincerely entertain the learning of the lesson of self-restraint by his pupils. This is because he knows it very well that all education teaches the highest lesson of spiritualism — to be good, bold and honest and to live straight to be true to the All Beautiful. To fulfil this objective of spiritualism, Gandhi humbly submits his viewpoints as a teacher as follows :

> It would be idle for me, if I were a liar, to teach boys to tell truth. A cowardly teacher would never succeed in making his boys valiant and a stranger to self-restraint could never teach his pupils the value of self-restraint. I saw, therefore, that I must be an eternal object lesson to the boys and girls living with me. They thus became my teachers, and I learnt I must be good and live straight if only for their sakes, I may say that the increasing discipline and restraint I imposed on myself at Tolstoy Farm was mostly due to those wards of mine.
>
> — M.K. Gandhi : *An Autobiography, op. cit.,* p. 414

To be self-restrained and pure in thought, word and deed is as Gandhi believes and translates into reality in his own life, to be on the threshold of an indescribable aura of spiritualism. The vision of the All Beautiful becomes a hallowed reality. How can one have this spiritual vision? Gandhi's categorical answer is to serve mankind is to sense God and to serve God thus is to pave the surest avenue of inner spiritual awakening and efflorescence. As an unparalleled apostle of the ascent of spiritualism, he characteristically remarks :

> Man's ultimate aim is the realization of God, and all his activities, social, political, religious, have to be guided by the ultimate aim of the vision of God. The immediate service of all human beings becomes a necessary part of the endeavour, simply because the only way to find God is to see Him in his creation and be one with it. This can only be done by service of all. I am a part and parcel of the whole, and I cannot find Him apart from the rest of humanity. My countrymen are my nearest neighbours. They have become so helpless, so resourceless, so inert that I must concentrate myself on serving them. If I could persuade myself that I should find Him in a Himalayan cave, I would proceed there immediately. But I

> know that I cannot find Him apart from humanity.
>
> — M.K. Gandhi : *Harijan*, August 29, 1936

The unison of mankind as one and indivisible that actually serves as the core of spiritualism finds a vivid exposure in Gandhian spiritualism. As Gandhi clearly states,

> I believe in absolute oneness of God and therefore also of humanity. What though we have many bodies? We have but one soul. The rays of the sun are many through refraction. But they have the same source.
>
> — M.K. Gandhi : *Young India*, September 25, 1924

Again,

> I do not believe that an individual may gain spiritually and those that surround him suffer. I believe in *advaita*. I believe in the essential unity of man for that matter of all that lives. Therefore I believe that if one man gains spiritually, the whole world gains with him and if one man fails, the whole world fails to that extent.
>
> *Ibid.*

To boost spiritualism in mankind is, as Gandhi believes, to promote the spirit of oneness, and to promote this spirit is to promote the inherent spirit of love. Unless love takes the upper hand in the history of mankind, spiritualism hardly thrives in a strife-torn world. Man loses the spirit of the soul-force nursled in the spirit of love. As Gandhi observes,

> The fact that there are so many men still alive in the world shows that it is based not on the force of arms but on the force of truth or love. Therefore, the greatest and most unimpeachable evidence of the success of this force is to be found in the fact that, in spite of the wars of the world, it still lives on.
>
> Thousands, indeed tens of thousands, depend for this existence on a very active working of this force. Little quarrels of millions of families in their daily lives disappear before the exercise of this

> force. Hundreds of nations live in peace. History does not and cannot take note of this fact. History is really a record of every interruption of the even working of the force of love or of the soul. Two brothers quarrel; one of them repents and reawakens the love that was lying dormant in him; the two again begin to live in peace; nobody takes note of this. But if the two brothers, through the intervention of solicitors or some other reason take up arms or go to law — which is another form of the exhibition of brute force — their doings would be immediately noticed in the press, they would be the talk of their neighbours and would probably go down in history. And what is true of families and communities is true of nations. There is no reason to believe that there is one law for families and another for nations. History, then, is a record of an interruption of the course of nature. Soul-force, being natural, is not noted in history.
>
> — M.K. Gandhi : *Hind Swaraj or Indian Home Rule*, Navajivan Publishing House, Ahmedabad, 1944. p. 45.

Spiritualism, being an ideal and natural force in the form of love that needs no reference in the pages of history, prepares mankind for greater and nobler advancements in the pursuit of Truth. It is Truth that eternally conveys what mankind should strive for and how this beautiful world of ours can be turned into an elegant abode of the All Beautiful. When Gandhi speaks of this eternal poignance of Truth, he delves deep into the spiritual essence of humanism to heighten the endless endeavour of man to exceed himself towards greater and purer excellence. The littleness of day to day life finds hardly any room for any strong foothold. The agonies and anxieties looming gravely over the existence of humanity are quietened and transformed into challenges for a glorious revival of spiritualism. How does the process actually find its avenue of manifestation? How does a person rise above oddities in legion? For Gandhi, the answers are not far to seek for whenever there is a dynamism in man that caters to creative and constructive thinking all the oddities are erased out of the firmament of the mind like stray clouds that are swept away with the gushing wind. In fact, the ascent of man starts with this inner aura of consciousness that thrives from life beyond life.

Admittedly, the ascent of man and spiritualism deserves a qualitative change in self-satisfaction. It is an acid rest for an individual to win over his littleness by means of all earnest endeavour and to be hallowed with the inner light of erudition and self-sacrifice that stands for true spiritualism. Gandhi makes a characteristic exposition in this connection :

> When self-satisfaction creeps over a man, he has ceased to grow and therefore has become unfit for freedom. He who offers a little sacrifice from a lowly and religious spirit quickly realizes the littleness of it. Once on the path of sacrifice, we find out the measure of our selfishness and must continually wish to give more and not be satisfied till there is a complete surrender.
>
> — M.K. Gandhi : *Young India*, September 29, 1921.

What Gandhi primarily emphasizes on the ascent of man and spiritualism is a continual and devoted endeavour to reduce himself to a cipher or a zero. This is the golden means to attain Truth — *tapasya* unending to usher forth the aura of true spiritualism. This is the ultimate vision of God that represents the highest endeavour of humanity. Gandhi characterizes Truth as 'the right designation of God' on this spiritual excellence of mankind. When man ceases to be selfish and ardently strives for continual self-surrender he completely diminishes his aspiration for self-interest and merges in the spiritual beauty of the All Beautiful. It may be that all persons have not the same avenue of searching truth. The strategies for Truth to be endeared might be different and might also vary. But, then, Truth remains unchanged in case of spiritual unison of man and the All Beautiful. Gandhi makes a very significant and poignant exposition :

> Does not God Himself appear to different individuals in different aspects? Still we know that He is one. But Truth is the right designation of God. Hence there is nothing wrong in everyone following Truth according to his lights. Indeed it is his duty to do so. Then if there is a mistake on the part of anyone to so following Truth, it will be automatically set right. For the quest of Truth involves *tapas* — self-suffering, sometimes even unto death. There can be no place in it for even a trace of self-interest. In such selfless search for Truth nobody can lose his bearings for long.
>
> — M.K. Gandhi : *From Yeravda Mandir, op. cit.,* p.4.

The birth of man is an enigma and askance for spiritual excellence. He is born perhaps to justify that the birth for him is an experience of the self in multidimensional avenues to be mingled with the Spirit Eternal — the Supreme Self. For him the littleness and desolation of experience and emotion, understanding and appreciation are the flimsy veils of poignance and depth of vision. The real birth of man is the birth of a new awakening, a new insight, a new light of spiritualism. The birth of *Karuna* is the ascent of man and spiritualism. Is the Holy grail a beckoning reality or a myth man made or otherwise? Gandhi gives the answer to remember and rethink for ever.

2

SPIRITUAL EDUCATION: Gandhian Viewpoints

Education is always an askance and enquiry. It is an introspection, a look within, a look to visualize and revisualize the 'man' in man. For Gandhi, education is more than an askance and enquiry. It is more than than bare introspection or even revisualization. It is an insight ceaseless, unending. It is, furthermore, an insight within insight or, better an insight for the beyonding of consciousness. For this Gandhi allows no compartmentalization between education and spiritualism. He discards the division between the two because, according to him, the true pursuit of education is nothing but that of spiritualism.

How does Gandhi arrive at the conclusion that education and spiritualism allow no difference between the two? The answer is not very far to seek nor is it very difficult to understand. In his own simple exposition, Gandhi ensures the fact that education aims at revelation and assimilation of truth that forms an inseparable and obligatory part of spiritualism. When one accepts the fact that God is Truth or Love one cannot but accept the component of education — Truth or Love. Gandhi further accentuates the union between education and spiritualism as follows:

> If God is love, God is above all, truth *** Two years ago, however, I went a step further and said ; "Truth is God".
>
> — M.K. Gandhi : *Young India,* December 31, 1931.

The experience of spiritualism as Gandhi strongly advocates is an impossibility unless there is a disciplined approach to training in spiritual education. He has himself allowed to have the experience of spiritual education in association with the boys at the Tolstoy Farm. Consequently, this experience has taught him how to be enriched with the education for spiritual development.

That spiritual education ensures boldness and awareness to impose restrictions not with crude imposition of law and order but with a certain sense of spiritual insight is obvious. Here is Gandhi's own experience:

> A coward teacher would never succeed in making his boys valiant, and a stranger to self-restraint could never teach his pupils the value of self-restraint. I saw, therefore, that I must be an eternal object lesson to the boys and girls living with me. They thus became my teachers, and I learnt I must be good and live straight if only for their sakes I may say that the increasing discipline and restraint I imposed on myself at Tolstoy Farm was mostly due to those wards of mine.
>
> One of them was wild, unruly, given to lying, and quarrelsome. On one occasion, he broke out most violently. I was exasperated. I never punished my boys, but this time I was very angry. I tried to reason with him. But he was adamant and even tried to over reach me. At last I picked up a ruler lying at hand and delivered a blow on his arm. I trembled as I struck him. I dare say he noticed it. This was an entirely novel experience for them all. The boy cried out and begged to be forgiven. He cried out because the beating was painful to him; he could, if he had been so minded, have paid me back in the same coin, being a stoutly built youth of seventeen, but he realized my pain in being driven to this violent resource. Never again after this incident die he disobey me. But I still repent that violence. I am afraid I exhibited before him that day not the spirit, but the brute, in me.
>
> I have always been opposed to corporal punishment. I remember only one occasion on which I physically punished one of my sons. I have therefore never until this day been able to decide whether I was right or wrong in using the ruler. Probably it was improper, for it was prompted by anger and a desire to punish. Had it been an expression only of my distress, I should have considered it justified. But the motive in this case was mixed.

—M.K. Gandhi : *An Autobiography,* Navajivan Publishing House, Ahmedabad, 1941, pp. 414-15.

Again,

> Cases of misconduct on the part of the boys often occurred after this, but I never resorted to corporal punishment. Thus in my endeavour to impart spiritual training to the boys and girls under me, I came to understand better and better the power of the spirit.
>
> —*Ibid.* p. 415.

Spiritual education and for that end in view the exercise of the spirit can, therefore, be imparted in the training of the spirit. And, as stated above, the teacher has a very significant role to play. Indeed, it is the teacher who alone by being a living example to his pupil can instil the lesson of spiritualism most effectively. As Gandhi remarks :

> Just as physical training was to be imparted through physical exercise, even so the training of the spirit was possible only through the exercise of the spirit. And the exercise of the spirit entirely depended on the life and character of the teacher. The teacher had always to be mindful of his p's and q's, whether he was in the midst of his boys or not.
>
> —*Ibid.* pp. 414.

The idea that spiritual education is impossible for pupils because they are not matured enough is erroneous, has been proved by Gandhi in his thoughts and experiments on spiritual education. He, of course, does not ignore that it is very difficult to impart spiritual education to any boys and girls because they hardly allow themselves to be serious in having or undergoing such type of education of training. Moreover, it is also very difficult to train them to differentiate between religious and spiritual education. This necessarily hampers self-realization and self-activity, if not properly guided in the training of character and discipline. The culture of the spirit among the pupil-community, therefore, needs a new approach in all our educational plans and programmes. Gandhi makes a very fine analysis:

> The spiritual training of the boys is a much more difficult matter than their physical and mental training. I relied little on religious

> books for the training of the spirit. Of course I believed that every student should be acquainted with the elements of his own religion and have a general knowledge of his own scriptures, and therefore, I provided for such knowledge as best as I could. But that, to my mind, was part of the intellectual training. Long before I undertook the education of the youngsters of the Tolstoy Farm I had realized that the training of the spirit was a thing by itself. To develop the spirit is to build character and to enable one to work towards a knowledge of God and self-realization. And I held that this was an essential part of the training of the young, and that all training without culture of the spirit was of no use, and might be even harmful.
>
> *Ibid*., p. 417.

As a practical teacher of education for spiritualism, Gandhi knows it very well that the pupils should be trained and oriented in spiritual education in their young age. This is the best period when education for spiritual development is best imparted. The idea of self-realization also gets a favourable avenue of manifestation. As Gandhi remarks:

> I am familiar with the superstition that self-realization is possible only in the fourth stage of life i.e. *Sannyasa* (renunciation). But it is matter of common knowledge that those who defer preparation for this invaluable experience until the last stage of life attain not self-realization but old age amounting to a second and pitiable childhood, living as a burden on this earth. I have a full recollection that I have held these views even whilst I was teaching i.e., in 1911-12, though I might not then have expressed them in identical language.
>
> —*Ibid.*

What are the strategies for imparting spiritual education to our young boys and girls? What, again, should be the role of teachers in doing so? As an ardent promoter of spiritual education, Gandhi prescribes for the training of the spirit not merely theoretically but also practically. In fact, he strongly emphasizes on the life and character of the teacher himself, which forms an inseparable part of spiritual education. If the teacher, as he categorically asserts, fails to set a living example of spiritual education by means of his mode of living and character, no spiritual attainment is possible for pupils. They fail to be disciplined in their day to day life and lack in having and exercising the invaluable quality of self-restraint. In this connection, the Gandhian strategies and view-points of imparting spiritual education are very significant:

> I made the children memorize and recite hymns, and read to them from books on moral training. But that was far from satisfying me. As a I came into closer contact with them I saw that it was not through books that one could impart training of the spirit. Just as physical training was to be imparted through physical exercise, and intellectual through intellectual exercise, even so the training of the spirit was possible only through the exercise of the spirit. And the exercise of the spirit entirely depended on the life and character of the teacher. The teacher had always to be mindful of this p's and q's whether he was in the midst of his boys or not.
>
> It is possible for a teacher situated miles away to affect the spirit of the pupils by his way of living. It would be idle for me, if I were a liar, to teach boys to tell the truth. A cowardly teacher would never succeed in making his boys valiant, and a stranger to self-restraint could never teach his pupils the value of self-restraint. I saw, therefore, that I must be an eternal object-lesson to the boys and girls living with me. They thus became my teachers.
>
> —*Ibid.*, p. 418.

With education as the mainspring for spiritual development, Gandhi stresses on education for right thinking. He, therefore, upholds the view that if pupils are encouraged to disseminate between the right and wrong, the good and the evil, the moral and the immoral, truth and untruth, they will be able to form within themselves the rightest attitude towards spiritualism. Books, then, will hardly replace the finer spiritual sensibilities or the head and the heart in them. Gandhi's own view on how to enable pupils to have spiritualism by means of training to think deserves our attention:

> Pupils should know to discriminate between what should be

> received and what rejected. It is the duty of the teacher to teach his pupils discrimination. If we go on taking in indiscriminating we would be no better than machines. We are thinking, knowing beings and we must in this period distinguish truth from untruth, sweet from bitter language, clean from unclean thing, and so on. But the student's path today is strewn with more difficulties than the one of distinguishing good from bad things. The *rishis* taught their pupils without books. They only gave them a few *mantras* which the pupils treasured in their memories and translated in practical life. The present day student has to live in the midst of heaps of books, sufficient to choak him.
>
> — M.K. Gandhi : *Young India*, January 29, 1925.

What, then, is the true goal of education? What, according to Gandhi, is spiritualism in relation to education? It is, as he categorically states, 'the making of the whole man', the man who eliminates all crude facts of life and enriches the broader visions and finer sensibilities within him. As a student, it is the duty of every one to endlessly strive towards harmonization of body, mind and soul and uphold the true, the good and the beautiful. The whole pattern of education, as Gandhi earnestly feels, should be directed towards spiritual realization which is 'the true economics of education'. All education is self-realization which ultimately rewards one with the realization of the Supreme Being, the All Beautiful, All True or All Good. The education of the heart is therefore of primary importance and this education should be introduced right from beginning of childhood. Gandhi elucidates such type of spiritual education very characteristically:

> The baneful effects of absence of proper co-ordination and harmony among the various faculties of body, mind and soul respectively are obvious. They are all around us; only we have lost perception of them owing to our present perverse associations. Take the case of our village folk, from their childhood upward they toil and labour in their fields from morning till night like their cattle in the midst of whom they live. Their existence is a weary endless round of mechanical drudgery unrelieved by a spark of intelligence or higher grace of life. Deprived of all scope for developing their mind and soul, they have sunk to the level of the beast,

Life to them is a sorry bungle which they muddle through anyhow. On the other hand, what goes by the name of education in our schools and colleges in the cities today is in reality only intellectual dissipation. Intellectual training is there looked upon as something altogether unrelated to manual or physical work. But since the body must have some sort of physical exercise to keep it in health, they vainly try to attain that end by means of an artificial and otherwise barren system of physical culture which would be ridiculous beyond words if the result was not so tragic. The young man who emerges from this system can in no way compete in physical endurance with an ordinary labourer. The slightest physical exertion gives him headache; a mild exposure to the sun is enough to cause him giddiness. And what is more, all this is looked upon as quite 'natural'. As for the faculties of the heart, they are simply allowed to run to seed or to grow anyhow in a wild undisciplined manner. The result is moral and spiritual anarchy. And it is regarded as something laudable.

— M.K. Gandhi: *Harijan,* May 8, 1937.

To save the learner from 'moral and spiritual anarchy' with which modern education is blissfully ignorant is the fundamental goal of Gandhian spiritualism in education. And, for this, Gandhi makes a clear analysis of the child who is stored towards the education of the heart — the education that practically spells out spiritualism:

Supposing he (the child) is set to some useful occupation like spinning, carpentry, agriculture etc., for his education, and in that connection is given a thorough comprehensive knowledge relating to the theory of the various operations that he is to perform and use and construction of the tools that he would be wielding. He would not only develop a fine, healthy body but also a sound vigorous intellect that is not merely academic but is firmly rooted in and is tested from day today experience. His intellectual education would include a knowledge of mathematics and the various sciences that are useful for an intelligent and efficient exercise of his avocation. If to this is added literature by way of recreation, it would give him a perfect, well-balanced, all-round education in which the intellect, the body and the spirit have all full play and develop together into a natural, harmonious whole. Man is

> neither mere intellect, nor the gross animal body, nor the heart or soul alone. A proper and harmonious combination of all the three is required for the making of the whole man and constitutes the true economics of education.
>
> —*Ibid.*

For such a 'true economics of education' as Gandhi illustrates in connection with the role of spiritualism in education, the essential components of education of the whole man necessitates a re-thinking. The lesson that the power of the human spirit is the greatest power on earth is taught by Gandhi as a great exponent of spiritualism. As Radhakrishnan remarks,

> Wars are caused by the passions in our heart, by the blind, black, uncontrollable greed in us. Each one of us has to fight the battle within himself. Kurukshetra is within us. Each one of us has to decide between love which saves the world and hate which destroys it. We have to purify ourselves by our effort and save others by our action, Gandhiji acquired the chastity of these consecrated to truth whose power is matchless by the practice of fasts, prayers and vows. Gandhiji occupies an important place in the spiritual evolution of mankind. He speaks to us of the promised land, the goal of our endeavour. Though some of us may not enter it we have to strive for it and salute it from afar. Whenever we think of Gandhiji, let us remember that the power of the human spirit is mightier than the mightiest bomb.
>
> — Sarvepalli Radhakrishnan : *Occasional Speeches and Writings,* Publications Division, Ministry of Information and Broadcasting, Government of India, Third Series, July 1959-May 1962, December 1963, p. 274.

The education that enables the child to have a control over passions and emotions, greatly demands a greater priority, a far more serene consciousness for the modern mind already maimed and crippled at the hands of automation and passivity. For true education, the education of the intellect cannot but be synchronized with the education of how to utilize the bodily organs in the best possible way. And, for this, the spiritual development of the child necessitates proper manifestation. Gandhi elucidates this view as follows:

> True education of the intellect can only come through a proper exercise and training of the bodily organs, e.g. hands, feet, eyes, ears, nose, etc. In other words, an intelligent use of the bodily organs in a child provides the best and quickest way of development of his intellect. But unless the development of the mind and the body goes hand in hand with a corresponding awakening of the soul, the former alone would prove to be a poor lopsided affair. By spiritual training I mean education of the heart. A proper and all-round development of the mind, therefore, can take place only when it proceeds *pari passu* with the education of the physical and spiritual faculties of the child. They constitute an indivisible whole. According to this theory, therefore, it would be a gross fallacy to suppose that they can be developed piecemeal or independently of one another.
>
> — M.K. Gandhi : *Harijan,* May 8, 1937.

The poem to be written in course of education by means of spiritual development is not a myth. And the history of human civilization and human excellence cannot but admit the fact that it is Gandhi and Gandhi alone who has ennobled manual work as the highest spiritual endeavour in education. Accordingly, the culture of the brain must thrive with the culture of hands and feet — the culture that makes a balance between intellect and spirit. Moreover, the question of communicated education which ensures the education of the heart is also emphasized in the Gandhian strategies for education for spiritual excellence. What Gandhi actually strives forth to achieve this objective is to bring about a definite revolutionary approach to education by means of an ashramic mode of living for pupils who will lead a spiritual life in an ideal environment. The society in which such an endeavour takes place can cherish the spiritual fulfilment as badly needed. In fact, the very concept of his Basic education is formulated and worked out for this end in view:

> He (Gandhi) had great regard for what could be achieved with men's hands and feet. Indeed he used to say, 'There is no point in developing the brain only. One has to develop one's brain through one's hands'. If I were a poet, I would write a beautiful poem on

> the possibilities of the five fingers of one's hand. Those who do not know how to use their hands get little profit out of education. They are like one who sings false notes without feeling the music. Books are never sufficiently interesting to hold the interest of the mind. The mind begins to wonder. Only manual work brings you back to reality. **** Today one tends to say that a person is cultured if he does not use his hands. It is necessary to correct the concept of culture and spirituality and recognize and embellish the moral and spiritual equalities of the different occupations of the working classes. And that was for Gandhi completely right.
>
> — Anibal del Campo : 'Application of truth and non-violence in Gandhiji's teaching and work', Quoted from *Truth and Nonviolence: A Unesco Symposium on Gandhi*, Ed. by T.K. Mahadevan, Gandhi Peace Foundation, New Delhi 1970, pp. 198-199.

As regards spiritual education to eliminate and replace sexual passion among young learners in educational institutions, Gandhi has a very practical approach to soul enlivening education. Let the education of the heart be imparted by means of enabling and encouraging learners to think of nobler and higher values and norms of life. Let them be continually stimulated to awaken the soul in all purity and freshness, simplicity and politeness. Then the coils of passion will become loose and fragile and will no longer be able to divert humane sensibilities towards evil directions. As a promoter of such type of education for spiritualism, Gandhi, therefore, advocates for sublimation of sexual passions through dissemination of a clear concept of right and wrong, good and evil. As he significantly remarks,

> We cannot properly control or conquer the sexual passion by turning a blind eye to it. I am, therefore, strongly in favour of teaching young boys and girls the significance and right use of their generative organs and in my own way I have tried to impart this knowledge to young children of both sexes, for whose training I was responsible. But the sex education that I stand for must have for its object the conquest and sublimation of the sex passion. Such education should automatically serve to bring home to children the essential distinction between man and brute, to make them realize that it is man's special privilege and pride to be gifted with the faculties of head and heart both, that he is a think-

ing no less than a feeling animal, and to renounce the sovereignty of reason over the blind instinct is, therefore, to renounce a man's estate. In man, reason quickens and guides the feeling, in brute, the soul lies ever dormant. To awaken the heart is to awaken the dormant soul, the awaken reason and to inculcate discrimination between goo1 and evil. Today, our entire environment — our reading, our thinking and our social behaviour — is generally calculated to subserve and cater for the sex age. To break through its encoils is no easy task. But it is a task worthy of our highest endeavour.

— D.G. Tendulkar : *Mahatma,* Publications Division, Ministry of Information and Broadcasting, Government of India, Vol. IV, p. 62.

To eliminate "sex complex" from society is the most important task to be taken up and performed right from educational institutions where children should, as Gandhi strongly believes, be taught how to lead a desirable moral and spiritual life. The soul force in every learner requires a disciplined exercise in the lesson of spirtual awakening. Otherwise passion takes the upper hand and the whole country becomes an easy victim to greed and lust, corruption and sensualism. The great warning against extinction of man as man, as the most sanctified personality is that of preservation and nursling of the soul-force which, in other words, represents manifestation of spiritual education. Gandhi characteristically high-lights sex education from the above spiritual ends in view:

Sex complex is today steadily gaining ground in India. And what is more, those who fall under its sway feel as if there is something meritorious about it. When a slave begins to take pride in his fetters and hugs them like precious ornaments, the triumph of the slave-owner is complete. But this success of cupid, spectacular though it may be, will, I am convinced, prove to be short-lived and ignorable,and at long last, will end in inanition even like a scorpion whose venom is spent. But that does not mean that we can in the meantime afford to sit in folded hands. The certainty of its defeat need not, must not, lull us into a false sense of security. The conquest of lust is the highest endeavour of a man's or a woman's existence. And without overcoming lust, man cannot hope to rule over self; without rule over self, there can be no

> *swaraj* or *Ram Raj*. Rule of all without the rule of oneself would prove to be as deceptive and as disappointing as a painted toy mango, charming to look at, but hollow and empty within. No worker who has not overcome lust, can hope to render any genuine service to the cause of the Harijans, communal unity, *Khadi*, cow protection or village reconstruction. Great causes like these cannot be served by intellectual equipment alone, they call for spiritual effort or soul-force. Soul-force comes only through God's grace and never descends upon a man who is a slave to lust.
>
> —*Ibid.*, pp. 62-63.

As an ardent exponent of spiritualism, Gandhi thinks that the lesson of controlling animal passions sincerely and steadfastly heightens one towards spiritual excellence. Side by side with the restraint of animal passions, one should also be always on the alert to safeguard moral laws and principles. Such type of awareness will guide one to explore the finer spiritual nuances of life. As Gandhi observes,

> It is wrong and immoral to seek to escape the consequences of one's acts. It is good for a person who over-eats to have an ache and a fast. It is bed for him to indulge his appetite and then escape the consequences by taking tonics or other medicines. It is still worse for a person to indulge in his animal passions and escape the consequences of his acts. Nature is relentless and will have full revenge for any such violation of her laws. Moral results can only be produced by moral restraints. All other restraints defeat the very purpose for which they are intended.
>
> — R.K. Prabhu & U.R. Rao (Compiled) : *The Mind of Mahatma Gandhi,* Oxford University Press, 1945. p. 108.

To accelerate creative education in course of basic education for humanizing and spiritualizing the inner visions of life has some definite points of departure of which the march of man towards higher and nobler endeavour deserves distinction. Gandhi points out his educational objectives from these specific aims of education. In fact, his exposure on Basic Education throws light on the spiritual dimension of education:

> I am grateful that so many educationists have blessed the new scheme. There have been critics also; but when I launched the scheme I did not know that it would appeal to anyone beyond the circle of my co-workers. When I consider the masses of India and the masses situated as they are, I could not think of any other type of education. With them work must precede anything else, and the concern of an educationist is to make that work educative.
>
> Let every child feel that he creates something for use and also expands his mind and heart there-through.
>
> — D.G. Tendulkar: *Mahatma, op. cit.,* p. 200.

As a great initiator of the theory of work as worship that embodies spiritualism, Gandhi wants to bring about a new pattern of education that fosters a broadening of the mind along with a widening of spiritual outlook. For this, his programmes for Basic Education maintain a synchronization of the high and the low, the rich and the poor, the advantaged and the disadvantaged in the society. The central idea of his new scheme of education for moral and spiritual regeneration of mankind brings forth this objective as elucidated by him:

> My idea is not merely to teach a particular profession of occupation to children, but to develop the full man through teaching that occupation. He will not only learn weaving, for instance, but learn why he should weave in a particular fashion and not any other, why he should handle yarn in a particular fashion and no other, and why he should himself know spinning and why should insist on a particular count for a particular kind of weaving. All these things the weaver boy does not learn at home. The spinning wheel is to him just what it was a thousand years ago. We make him learn the art of making the most efficient wheel and a loom, not so as to displace other labour but so as to make them more efficient than the existing models. * * * * For, I want to bring about equalization of status. The working classes have all these centuries been isolated and relegated to the lower status. They have been Shudras, and the word has been interpreted to mean an inferior status. I want to allow no differentiation between the son of a weaver, of an agriculturist and of a school master.
>
> —*Ibid.*, pp. 200-201.

The education of the whole man, as Gandhi sincerely believes, begins with the education of sympathy — the education that relieves the little 'I' and exposes the great 'We'. This lesson of togetherness or oneness is the greatest lesson of spiritualism for unison of man and the All Beautiful. Therefore, the knowledge and experience of every human being is purified and spirituality solemnized in the service of mankind. Gandhi characteristically explains this viewpoint as follows:

> If I were a perfect man, I own, I should not feel the miseries of neighbours as I do. As a perfect man I should take note of them, prescribe a remedy, and compel adoption by the force of unchallengeable truth in me. But as yet I only see as through a glass darkly and therefore have to carry conviction by slow and laborious processes, and then, too, not always with success. **** I would be less human if, with all my knowledge of the unavoidable misery pervading the land * * * * I did not feel with and for all the suffering of the dumb millions of India.
>
> — Pyarelal : *Mahatma Gandhi : The Last Phase,* Navajivan Publishing House, Ahmedabad, 1958, p. 324.

A revolution in education through spiritual efflorescence as the modern world badly demands right now or never can alone proclaim the victory of man. But unless the inner conscience — the spiritual forté — of everyone is enkindled, education loses its real identity in the exposure of nothingness. Education, therefore, awaits 'the still small voice within' as Gandhi looks upon it from the spiritual point of view. Of course, his firm conviction on the awakening of good sense and sensibilities of every human being even at the cost of life marks a new avenue of significance of spiritualism. As he poignantly observes,

> I want to declare to the world that, whatever may be said to the contrary, and although I might have forfeited the regard and even the trust of many in the West — and I bow my head low — but ever for their friendship or their love, I must not suppress that voice within, call it conscience, call it the promoting of my inner basic nature. There is something within me impelling me to cry out my agony. I have known exactly what it is. That something in me which never deceives me tells me now : 'You may have to stand against the whole world although you may have to stand

> alone. You have to stare the world in the face although the world may look at you with blood-shot eyes. Do not fear. Trust that little thing in you which resides in the heart and says : Forsake friends, wife, all; but testify to that for which you have lived and for which you have to die.'
>
> — R.K. Prabhu and U.R. Rao (Compiled) : *op. cit.*, p. 16.

To penetrate deep into one's conscience as Gandhi prescribes for education for spiritualism has its foundation on right doing, right feeling and right thinking. Such type of education is education for continual growth and development or, in other words, education for fulness. Such type of education, again, builds a strong spiritual foundation by means of incorporating and inculcating the education of character. How can a learner be inspired to have the spiritual lesson of education for character building? According to Gandhi, a learner should first and foremost be stimulated in maintaining and fostering purity in personal life through observance of *brahmacharya*. As he significantly observes,

> Purity of personal life is the one indepensable condition for building a sound education. And my meetings with thousands of students and the correspondence which I continuously have with students, in which they pour out their innermost feelings and take me into their confidence, show me quite clearly that there is much left to be desired, I am sure that all of you understand thoroughly what I mean. In our languages there is a beautiful word, equivalent for the word student, that is *brahmachari*. *Vidyarthi* is a coined word and a poor equivalent of *brahmachari*. And I hope you know what the word *brahmachari* means. It means searcher after God, one who conducts himself so as to bring himself nearest to God in the least possible time. And all the great religions of the world, however much they differ, are absolutely one on this fundamental thing that no man or woman with an impure heart can possibly appear before the Great White Throne. All our learning or recitation of the *Vedas*, correct knowledge of Sanskrit, Latin, Greek and what not will avail us nothing if they do not enable us to cultivate absolute purity of heart. The end of all knowledge must be building up of character.
>
> — M.K. Gandhi : *Young India,* September 8, 1927.

The education for nearness to spiritualism, for making one worthy of beholding the 'Great White Throne' as Gandhi characteristically remarks, is indeed a search within, unending but thrilling and stimulating. As education is a search within it is an endeavour, lifelong and living, to find out greater and nobler possibilities for manifestation of purity and perfection. With all encumbrances and limitations the education that paves avenues of self-understanding and self-assessment is doubly blessed. First, it allows the mind to go ahead with newer visions and promises in life. Secondly, it allows the mind with all its possibilities of transcendence to be gifted with creative and aesthetic enjoyment and appreciation. Hence, spiritual education for purity and poignance, insight and perfection.

As a practical initiator of spiritualism, Gandhi leaves education wide open for inner awakening and purity of perfection. He maintains that unless a learner knows how to draw out his inherent spiritual force latent in him, the idea of self-understanding or self-appreciation becomes a myth. Moreover, the consequences of every endeavour for self-analysis or self-study thus ignored or winked at due to matter-of-fact, dull, drab, mechanical abstraction with which modern education is alarmingly camouflaged, lead him for away from the aura of transcedence as an invigorating symbol of spiritualism.

In the momentous sessions of the Education Conference at Wardha on October, 22, 1937, Gandhi highlights manual training in education right from the primary stage mainly because he is interested in the wholeness of education:

> I am convinced that the present system of primary education is not only wasteful, but is positively harmful. Most of the boys are lost to their parents and to the occupation to which they are born. They pick up evil habits, affect the urban ways and get a smattering of something which may be anything but education. What then should be the form of primary education? I think the remedy lies in educating them by means of vocational or manual training. I have some experience of myself, having trained my sons and other children on the Tolstoy Farm in South Africa through some manual training, that is, carpentry or shoe-making which I learned from Kallenbach, who had his training in Trappist Monastery.
>
> — D.G. Tendulkar : *Op. cit.*, p. 191.

For such wholeness of education to be achieved through an insight into manual labour hardly affects intellectual education as it is often misinterpreted. But the 'practical religion' learnt through self-help by learners from the early stage in educational institutions goes a long way in having a clear conscience of the inner worth of spiritualism. The sense of empathy as a great spiritual force for the all round excellence of mankind rather than bare sympathy stream-rolled in bare livelihood in the garb of artificiality has much more to contribute to self-sufficiency and self-help and that is why Gandhi ventilates his vision of spiritualism in a distinct pattern of exposition. As he observes,

> I have been accused of being opposed to literary training. Far from it, I simply want to show the way in which it should be given. The self-supporting aspect has also been attacked. It is said, whereas we should be expending millions on the primary education, we are going to exploit the children. It is also feared that there would be enormous waste. This fear is also falsified by experience. As for exploiting or burdening the children, I would ask whether it was burdening the child to save him from a disaster. *Takli* is a good enough toy to play with. It is no less a toy because it is a productive one. Even today children help their parents to a certain extent. * * * Whilst the child will be encouraged to spin and help his parents with agricultural jobs, he will also be made to feel that he does not belong only to his parents but also to the village and to the country, and that he must make some return to them. That is the only way. I would tell the ministers that they make the children helpless by doling out education to them. They would make them self-confident and brave by their playing for their education by their own labour. This system is to be common to all Hindus, Muslims, Parsis and Christians. Why do I not lay any stress on religious instruction, people ask. Because I am teaching them practical religion, the religion of self-help.
>
> —*Ibid.*, pp. 192-193.

The education of feeling for others near or distant rather than education for bare utilitarianism, which truly stands for nursling of spiritualism is the onward march for the education of being. As an exponent of spiritual excellence through education, Gandhi strongly intends to bring about a radical change in the concept of education as a great spiritual force. What is really of greater importance is not education for utilitarianism with which he is unduly and ignorantly charged, but education for right thinking, right feeling and right doing to eliminate passion and enrich detachment. Emancipation of the spirit dormant in trivialities of passion is always a prized outcome of education. Gandhi's own viewpoints prove this point better:

> My soul refuses to be satisfied so long as it is a helpless witness of a single wrong or a single misery. But it is not possible for me, a weak, frail, miserable being, to mend every wrong or to hold myself free of blame for all the wrong I see. The spirit in me pulls one way, the flesh in me pulls in the other direction. There is freedom from action of these two forces but that freedom is attainable only by slow and painful stages. I cannot attain freedom by a mechanical refusal to act but only by intelligent action in a detached manner. This struggle resolves itself into an incessant crucifixion of the flesh so that the spirit may become entirely free.
>
> — Pyarelal : *Mahatma Gandhi : op cit.,* p. 324.

The education for emancipation of the inherent spirit of an individual is the only education that can as Gandhi thinks, bring about a total change of the sad lot of humanity. Education *sans* this spiritual aim becomes absolutely meaningless because it turns into an agent of utilitarian fulfilment. For a proper and scientific reorientation of education with a view to achieving the spiritual objective of inner enrichment, Gandhi prescribes the following propositions to do away with the system of slavish pattern of education:

1. The present system of education does not meet the requirements of the country in any shape or form. English, having been made the medium of instruction in all the higher branches of learning, has created a permanent bar between the highly educated few and the uneducated many. It has prevented knowledge from percolating to the masses. The excessive importance given to English, has cast upon the educated class a burden which has maimed them mentally for life and made them strangers in their own land. The absence of vocational training has made the educated class almost unfit for productive work and has harmed them physically. Money

spent on primary education is a waste of expenditure, in as much as what little is taught is soon forgotten and has little or no value in terms of the villages or cities. Such advantage as is gained by the existing system of education is not gained by the chief tax payer, his children getting the least.

2. The course of primary education should be extended at least to seven years and should include the general knowledge gained up to the matriculation standard less English and plus a vocation.
3. For the all-round development of boys and girls, all training should so far as possible to given through a profit-yielding vocation. Or, in other words, vocations should serve a double purpose- to enable the pupil to pay for his tuition through the products of his labour, and at the same time to develop the whole man or woman in him or her through the vocation learnt at school.
4. * * * Universities will look after the whole of the field of education and will prepare and approve courses of studies in various departments of education. No private school should be run without the previous sanction of the respective universities. University charters should be given liberally to any body of persons of proved worth and integrity, it being always understood that the universities will not cost the state anything except that it will bear the cost of running a central education department.

— D.G. Tendulkar : *op. cit.*, pp. 197-98.

Such a concrete programme of activities for education of the whole man, the education that leads one to spiritual development, as envisaged by Gandhi is a harmonious blend of rigour and simplicity that teaches one to be worthy of oneself and towards others in a society. When Gandhi speaks for truth or non-violence it also encapsulates this spiritual ascent of man. Let every child grow up in an atmosphere of purity and self-consciousness, self-restraint and fearlessness. No other education can replace this objective because no other education can embrace ardour and adoration, labour and devotion for spiritual erudition that heightens the inherent and true spirit of religion:

His (Gandhi's) whole life symbolised the spirit of struggle — non-violence, undoubtedly — against all sorts of oppression and inequality, be it racial, colour, caste or class. He laid down concrete programmes as he saw his light. This active campaigning testifies that he wanted a structural change in the iniquitous social order and political set-up. His approach was indeed individual-moral, since he believed that the human heart held the key to all social and political dynamics; but then again, the individual — a morally regenerated individual — of his conception was not someone living in isolation from the society nor was it a conceptual category abstracted from the organic whole, i.e. the society. What is more important to note is that in a static society like India- "a community of obedience" as it was called — where life appeared as a fatalistically determined phenomenon, he, by his repudiation of the theory of permanent inelasticity of human nature, introduced a new element of dynamism in the field of human action. While no credit is due to him for any novelty in the concept of dynamic and active human nature (he did not in fact claim any originality for himself), the reaffirmation of this thinking was itself of much significance. Criticism may be made of his views about human nature from rationalist and materialist points of view and one may hold that the concrete man as an ensemble of social relations has received inadequate attention in comparison to his stress on ideal man; but that should not blind one's vision so as not to be able to grasp the point of departure for his philosophy — the individual : fearless, self-restrained and self-conscious. This insistence on the regeneration of the individual may be interpreted to have introduced the bourgeois concept of sovereignty of the individual (in that case, it is to be understood in a deep sociological sense and in no other sense), but it may be presumed that it served a necessary function for awakening the slumbering masses of India from their semi-comatic condition. Without a band of idealistically-inspired individuals, no movement for political emancipation or social reform could take its stride. The ascetic vigour and the puritan ethical discipline that a *Satyagrahi* was obliged to undergo was necessary for such a purpose. It was a *psychologically necessary basis* for action.

— Buddhadeva Bhattacharyya : *Evolution of the Political Philosophy of Gandhi,* Calcutta Book House, 1969, pp. 112-113.

The education of non-violence as Gandhi firmly believes and shows in action, is the education of spiritualism. It is the inner faith, a longing for the ultimate good of one and all. It never makes any unison with violent methods nor does it allow the mind to be crippled and dwarfed in motivated pressure. As good unending is always an outcome of non-violence, one's dealing with violence cannot but have the inherent basis on bringing about a total change in the form of Truth and Goodness. *This, in other words, means that the lesson of* non-violence is the lesson of winning violence by means of Truth and Goodness. The fact that all delusions of untruth and violence are the consequences of the ignorance of the inner light within every person, is often branded as cowardice and weakness that conceal the teaching of spiritualism. An uncompromising apostle of spiritualism, Gandhi holds out this fact explicitly :

> I do not believe in short-violent-cuts to success. * * * * However much I may sympathize with and admire worthy motives, I am an uncompromising opponent of violent methods even to serve the noblest of causes. There is, therefore, really no meeting ground between the school of violence and myself. But my creed of non-violence not only does not preclude me but compels me even to associate with anarchists and all those who believe in violence. But that association is always with the sole object of weaning them from what appears to me their error. For experience convinces me that permanent good can never be the outcome of untruth and violence.
>
> Even, if my belief is a fond delusion, it will be admitted that it is a fascinating delusion.
>
> — R.K. Prabhu & U.R. Rao : *The Mind of Mahatma Gandhi, op. cit.*, p. 126.

The education for upholding Truth as an invincible force of spiritualism as Gandhi advocates is based on an end means *vice-versa* relationship. But, then, the implicit awareness should always be there in mankind. It is the awareness that evil cannot lead goodness. Rather is it goodness that gradually eliminates evil. Gandhi, therefore, badly urges for the ideal lesson of spiritualism on a favourable healthy foundation or means. His own interpretation on the means to be identified and adhered to, is significant:

> If I want to cross the ocean, I can do so only by means of a vessel; if I were to use a cart for that purpose, both the cart and I would soon find the bottom. 'As is the God, so is the votary' is a maxim worth considering. Its meaning has been distorted and men have gone astray. The means may be likened to a seed, the end to a tree; and there is just the same invisible connexion between the means and the end as there is between the seed and the tree. I can not likely to obtain the result flowing from the worship of God by laying myself prostrate before Satan. If, therefore, anyone is there to say: 'I want to worship God; it does not matter if I do so by means of Satan', it would be set down as ignorant folly. We reap exactly as we sow.
>
> — M.K. Gandhi : *Hind Swaraj or Indian Home Rule, op. cit.,* pp. 51-52.

To be true to the above means of holding goodness under any circumstances as Gandhi advocates is the source-point of spiritualism in education. Hence, self-purification through education. This process of self-purification as he always emphasises, is a continual and strenuous process. But then this is the only way to bring about a real social revolution through education of the masses in a spiritual manner. In his own words,

> The spiritual weapon of self-purification, intangible as it seems, is the most potent means of revolutionizing one's environment and loosening external shackles. It works subtly and invisibly, it is an intense process though it might often seem a weary and long-drawn process; it is the straightest way to liberation, the surest and quickest and no effort can be too great for it. What it requires is faith—an unshakable mountainlike faith that flinches from nothing.
>
> — M.K. Gandhi : *Young India,* April 30, 1925.

Even when Gandhi speaks of socialism, the lesson of spiritualism is always there acting as an unavoidable and mandatory guide. The education of socialism is, therefore, the education of spiritualism which teaches the lesson of unity in diversity, and purity of thought and action. It also provides for an atmosphere of truth and non-violence. For a socialistic society, harbouring purity of mind and body — an essential component of spiritual development — is not merely desirable but also compulsory to establish true socialism. The ills of untruth, the sad consequences of hatred and violence and the crude desire for sustenance of ill-wills cannot be eliminated unless these are replaced by a holistic and spiritual endeavour by means of Truth and non-violence. In course of explaining the true nature and significance of socialism, Gandhi elucidates how the education of spiritualism in the forms of purity, truth and non-violence brings about true socialism:

> Socialism is a beautiful word and, so far as I am aware, in socialism all the members of the society are equal — none low, none high. In the individual body, the head is not high because it is the top of the body, nor are the soles of the foot low because they touch the earth. Even as members of the individual body are equal, so are the members of the society. This is socialism.
>
> In it the prince and the peasant, the wealthy and the poor, the employer and the employee are all on the same level. In terms of religion, there is no duality in socialism. It is all unity. Looking at society all the world over, there is nothing but duality or plurality. Unity is conspicuous by its absence. * * * * * In the unity of my conception there is perfect unity in the plurality of designs. In order to reach this state, we may not look on things philosophically and say that we need not make a move until all are converted to socialism. Without changing our life we may go on giving addresses, forming parties and hawk-like seize the game when it comes our way. This is no socialism. The more we treat it as game to be seized, the further it must recede from us.
>
> Socialism begins with the first convert. * * * This socialism is as pure as crystal. It, therefore, requires crystal-like means to achieve it. Impure means result in an impure end. Hence the prince and the peasants will not be equalled by cutting off the prince's head, nor can the process of cutting off equalise the employer and the employees. One cannot reach truth by untruthfulness. Truthful conduct alone can reach truth. * * * * Non-violence is embedded in truth and *vice versa.* Hence has it been said that they are faces of the same coin. Either is inseparable from the other. Read the coin either way — the spelling of words will be different; the value is the same. This blessed state is unat-

> tainable without perfect purity. Harbour impurity of mind and body and you have untruth and violence in you.
>
> — Pyarelal : *op. cit.*, pp. 140-41.

The education for elimination of impurity of mind and body rests heavily on a spiritual askesis : the grace of the All Beautiful. Gandhi seeks to attain that grace through observance of *brahmacharya* which carries an altogether different and spiritually vibrant connotation. The spirit of *brahmacharya* goes far beyond bare purity of body and mind. It is a great controlling factor of one's thoughts, words and deeds. Gandhi's explicit exposition is significant:

> I have been trying to follow *brahmacharya* consciously and deliberately since 1899. My definition of it is purity not merely of body but of both speech and thought also. With the exception of what must be regarded as one lapse, I can recall no instance, during more than thirty-six years' constant and conscious effort, of mental disturbances, such as I experienced during this illness. I was disgusted with myself. The moment the feeling came, I acquainted my attendants and the medical friends with my condition. They could give me no help. I expected none. I broke loose after the experience from the rigid rest that was imposed upon me. The confession of the wretched experience brought relief to me. I felt as if a great load had been raised from over me. It enabled me to pull myself together before any harm could be done. But what of the *Gita*? Its teaching is clear and precise. A mind that is once hooked to the Star of Stars becomes incorruptible. How far I must be from Him, He alone knows. Thank God, my vaunted mahatmaship has never fooled me. But this enforced rest has humbled me as never before. It has brought to the surface my limitations and imperfections.
>
> — M.K. Gandhi : *Harijan,* February 29, 1936.

For a beyonding of oneself by playing on rightly the 'chords of the human heart', Gandhi believes that the lesson of spiritualism goes a far way in harmonizing whatever is not in tune with reality. It is an endless endeavour, no doubt. But then, the inherent lesson of reality and truth for the welfare of one and all sustains for ever. This acts like a faith that never dies and man marches on with this ideal because he is proud of it. As Gandhi observes,

> The virtue of an ideal consists in its boundlessness. But although religious ideals must thus from their very nature remain unattainable by imperfect human beings, although by virtue of their boundlessness they may seem ever to recede farther and farther away from us, the nearer we go to them still they are closer to us than our very hands and feet because we are more certain of their reality and truth then even our own physical being. This faith in ideal constitutes real life, in fact, it is man's all in all.
>
> — M.K. Gandhi : *Young India,* November 22, 1928.

A new educational set up to stimulate the society as a great source of spiritual development accelerates Gandhi's social revolution. He always maintains the view that absence of the lesson of man as a spiritual being in the society takes an individual for away from the vision of the All Beautiful. For him it is the society that formulates a new theory of spiritual evolution.

The social ills that keep the inner sensibilities inert and inactive necessitate a major change for human worth and this can only take place when everyone in the society is keen to transform himself from petty interests towards societal development, national and global. The two-fold process of evolution backed by a spiritual aspiration after enrichment of the truth within brings about a radical change in the society where every one *does* really feel and react with the spurt of benevolence. The individual then, as Gandhi shows in experimentations, merges in the greater 'We' of the greater society. The dictum 'God is Truth' is slowly but surely turned or changed into 'Truth is God'. This indeed, is the lesson of spiritualism which teaches the Gandhian lesson that every piece of bread symbolises God's blessings as a reward for cultivation of social harmony. This social harmonization consequential to the attainment of spiritual evolution of man in having and endearing everyone as *daridranarayana* is the most desirable and prized education that at the same time negotiates both national and global social imperatives. Our national movements remain misunderstood and misinterpreted unless this spiritual impact on the lesson of freedom-struggle remains unexposed. As it is significantly observed,

The analysis of society that Gandhi made and the direction in which, on the basis of such analysis, he wanted it to move, as well as the methodology of change and revolution suggested by him, are all available to us even today. But they are available only in a rudimentary form; for some of them were really a part of the great experiment that he was conducting in search of his truth but which he had to leave half-way and half-done. While the blueprint that Gandhi wanted to prepare for determining the basis of the new society is yet to be completed by perspective social thinkers and scientists, it is necessary to remember that Gandhi's total scheme of social development was based on a two-fold stimulus. The reflex of the new set-up was thus provided by the social realities of his time, while the validity of his social scheme was drawn from a rationale of global development.

Gandhi's entire approach was thus societal in content. Although Gandhi reposed great faith in God and believed in the values of spirituality and ethics, his spirituality, his God and his ethics were all products of the social reality. It is interesting to observe the gradual evolution of Gandhi's position in this regard. There was a time when Gandhi had thought that God would provide all the social guidance necessary for the recovery of man and his soul from the oppressive social set-up. 'God is truth' had said Gandhi and it was to God, therefore, that he had called upon all seekers of societal truth or reality to turn themselves.

Later Gandhi revised his position and came to the conclusion that the social reality was itself God. 'Truth is God' said Gandhi in later years and indicted that he had found his God in the habitats of the poor, the daridranarayana. Gandhi's position became further clear when he said, in his Independence Day message to the country on 15th August, 1947, that 'God comes to the poor in the shape of bread'. This arbit of relationship that he had worked out between God, 'Truth' and social reality placed, as one sees, social reality in the most crucial position and made everything else subservient to it. Gandhi's main concern was, therefore, with truth-the supreme fact of life, one that has accounted for the total global reality of his times.

— Sugata Das Gupta : 'Truth and Nonviolence in Gandhi's Humanism'; *Truth and Nonviolence,* Gandhi Peace Foundation, New Delhi, 1970, pp. 340-341.

The education for understanding and appreciating a society with genuine spiritual involvement as Gandhi believes, can revolutionalize humanism with the inner spirit of man. His spiritual vision of education is, therefore, neither parochial nor compartmental but comprehensive and complementary to the evolution of man. Education, as a subtle means of inner spiritual excellence, is always developmental and this should always ensure the inner spirit of every item of work. The education of spinning or *charkha* is, therefore, highly symbolic and it primarily symbolizes man's craving for spiritual fulness in the forms of self-dependence, self-understanding, self-help and dignity of labour that ultimately throws open for a learner the lesson of truth, love and gracefulness of man as an unparalleled spiritual being. A society thus christened in the learning of the lesson of spiritualism by means of self-help and self-excellence is neither barely religious nor ethical but evolutional and transcendental.

The introduction of spinning or *charkha* as an inseparable and compulsory subject for education on the basis of spiritual evolution as stated above has also its strong foundation on the spirit of austerity that marks a great line of departure from aggression of utilitarianism, perhaps the greatest enemy of spiritual poignance. In fact, it is Gandhi, and perhaps Gandhi alone, who teaches the lesson of spiritualism by means of the education of austerity as a great challenge against the violently surging waves of utilitarianism. It is also equally significant that his vision of a real India emerges from the spirit of simplicity which he himself embodies in his loin cloth of a far-sighted *fakir*. The inner spirit of poignance and purity of thought and action that Gandhi wants to highlight in his diverse programmes of Basic Education has its end-in-view of spiritual excellence. The more a learner is devoted towards simplicity and austerity, the more is he free from passions and sentimentalism, narrowness of spiritual vision.

Gandhi makes an in-depth approach to spiritualism through the education of austerity primarily because in his vision of a new world of spiritual regeneration he cannot do away with the blessings of simplicity and austerity. The unabated differences between the high and the low, the rich and the poor, the advantaged and the disadvantaged, the fortunate and the hapless have accentuated the need for an immediate and greater cohesion of humanism. And, for this, the process of living in simplicity necessitates a thrust through the education of austerity. A reinterpretation of the basic values of life paves a sounder avenue of the efflorescence of the education for spiritualism. The spinning wheel, a symbolic spirit of spiritualism, as Gandhi introduces in his educational plans and programmes, is nothing but looking within for a revaluation of the basic values of life.

As an introspective visionary, Gandhi redirects religion towards the best possible manifestation of spiritualism. For learning the highest moral low, too, spiritualism takes the course of love for mankind under any circumstances. Gandhi, therefore, stimulates the lesson of morality, religion and spiritualism in a synchronized manner of simplicity and tolerance. Accordingly, all human endeavour should be geared to the pursuit of love for one and all. All endeavour, as he earnestly feels, should be directed towards that objective of education that practically teaches the lesson of endearment — the lesson that will ultimately establish the Kingdom of Righteousness on earth. The education thus imparted to the learner at any seat of learning will rejuvenate him to be truly spiritual in being a partner to glorify the spiritual ascent of man. *The Rama Raj* of Gandhi actually indicates this spiritual ascent of man. With such a spiritual ascent of man as highlighted by Gandhi in his strategies for education for spiritual development, religion takes a new pattern in learning the lesson of tolerance. A study of religion through tolerance as visualized and practised by him, allows on individual to know and modify the imperfections and limitations of religious beliefs and faith. The spiritual insight through the lesson of tolerance that an individual learner attains, effectively contributes to the manifestation of religion as a great transcendental force. Gandhi's own exposition of tolerance as a great educative and spiritual force opens a newer avenue of education for emergence of spiritualism:

> If we had attained the full vision of Truth, we would no longer be mere seekers, but have become one with God, for Truth is God. But being only seekers, we prosecute our quest, and are conscious of our imperfection. And if we are imperfect ourselves, religion as conceived by us must also be imperfect. We have not realized religion in its perfection, even as we have not realized God. Religion of our conception, being thus imperfect, is always subject to a process of evolution and reinterpretation. Progress towards Truth, towards God, is possible only because of such evolution. And if all faiths outlined by men are imperfect, the question of comparative merit does not arise. All faiths constitute a revelation

of Truth, but all are imperfect, and liable to error. Reverence for other faiths need not blind us to their faults. We must be keenly alive to the defects of our own faith also, yet to leave it on that account, but try to overcome those defects. Looking at all religions with an equal eye, we would not only not hesitate, but would think it our duty, to blend into our faith every acceptable feature of other faiths.

Even as a tree has a single trunk, but many branches and leaves, so there is on true and perfect Religion, but it becomes many, as it passes through the human medium.

The one Religion is beyond all speech. Imperfect men put it into such language as they can command, and their words are interpreted by other men equally imperfect. Whose interpretation is to be held to be the right one? Everybody is right from his own standpoints, but it is not possible that everybody is wrong. Hence the necessity of tolerance, which does not mean indifference to one's own faith, but a more intelligent and purer love for it. Tolerance gives us spiritual insight, which is as far from fanaticism as the north pole from the south.

— M.K. Gandhi : *From Yeravda Mandir, op. cit.,* p. 55.

The education of tolerance as an invaluable component for spiritual insight as Gandhi introduces through his indigenous pattern of education essentially aims at widening the mind and broadening the outlook of the learner. The leaner becomes an endless persuer of the unity of mankind through self-realization and self-development. He, therefore, upholds education as a sound but very subtle means for appreciating religion as the core of spiritual excellence. His educational principles are, therefore, oriented towards the spiritual spurt for highlighting one Religion — the religion that places man as the endless worshipper of Truth, Goodness and Beauty and turns religion into an efflorescence of all-embracing love for mankind.

What, then, serves as a fundamental source for Gandhian spiritualism in disseminating education as a vehicle for development of spiritual insight? How does Gandhi himself equip for the right type of education for promotion of spiritual insight? Perhaps the answers to questions as above can be had from an understanding and appreciation of Gandhi's adoration for the education of religion and spiritualism from the Indian perspective. In fact, his life-long *tapasya* for the all-round goodness of everyone everywhere is based on the teaching of the Upanishadic doctrine of seeking God in every entity. The great spiritual lesson that Gandhi wants to be disseminated through education is the lesson of *ananda* attained by means of pursuit of spiritual oneness of mankind. The insight that will work upon all minds through such type of education is based upon the fact that the world is beautiful and pleasant. And as it is beautiful and pleasant, its inhabitants are also beautiful and pleasant. As the teaching of the *Upanishad* reminds us:

> *Iyong prithivi sarveshang bhutunang madhu*
> *Asyai prithivyai sarvani bhutani madhu.*
>
> — *Vrihadaranyak Upanishad* 2.5.1.

The lesson of the Upanishad for a greater visualization of the endless vast — *bhuma* — also finds a newer manifestation in Gandhi's viewpoints on spiritual education. His vision of a new world of learning for effulgence of the All Beautiful allows the learner to welcome in the heart of hearts whatever adores erudition in the forms of transcendence and betterment. As a protagonist of spiritual education he goes beyond education for utilitarianism and allows every persuer of advancement of learning to be more serene and sombre in education through work that in the end turns out to be a worship or rather an humble spiritual endeavour. Here, then, is the flimsy cloud of misapprehension that Gandhian education is primarily utilitarian but this becomes clear and evident when the point of serenity is least ignored. Admittedly, Gandhi's programmes for spiritual education overcome the littleness of knowing, feeling and understanding apparently and highlight the glory of being that accelerated the beyonding of man. This kind of spiritual education places man at the centre of interest and prays for continual evolution of consciousness.

An introspective study of the Gandhian viewpoints of spiritual education as discussed above throws wide open the following parameters:

(i) Spiritual education in the true sense of the expression is the only education for the advancement of man as man.

(ii) Education is a mental process — complex, unique, unending. Hence, spiritual education that embraces all those attributes.

(iii) Education is essentially an activity- intrinsic as well as extrinsic. Education through work that symbolizes worship is a far superior activity since it harmonizes the matter with the spirit.

(iv) Education is a component for gradual but sanguine inner development. Since spiritual education accelerates this inner development, all education should be directed towards this end in view.

(v) Education is a passport to transcendence in every avenue of human progress. Spiritual education as Gandhi expounds, quickens this transcendence since it safeguards human values like conscience, love and tolerance.

(vi) Education highlights what is True, Good and Beautiful. Gandhi handles education with the strategic force of self-dependence and non-violence, that actually promotes man towards spiritual and aesthetic excellence.

In a world of miseducation blinding every mind with delusions and disappointment, the light of spiritual education as Gandhi has enkindled is yet to reach the dark ocean of ignorance.

Are we aware?

3

SARVODAYA AND SPIRITUALISM: Gandhian Exposures

The best in man suffers most and the best in man is always hidden. It always awaits a re-beginning, a rebirth, a reawakening. A sense of belongingness to everyone in order to be christened and enriched with the sense of belongingness to oneself is the surest way of being in the avenue of the best in man. Such a sense of belongingness, when assured of efflorescence in spontaneity, springs forth spiritualism in its most desirable manifestation.

Unlike other spiritual thinkers of the world, Gandhi makes a sound platform of spiritual effulgence on the very contemplations and actions of man. He theorizes spiritualism as the fundamental lesson of human awakening, for he believes strongly that man, however erroneous in his innumerable endeavour for purity and perfection, is the sole embodiment of spiritualism. In other words, where man is ignored and left apart, spiritualism in all its essence bids goodbye. As an inseparable component of man's march for better awakening and greater consciousness, it, therefore, forms an integral part of human life and activities.

What type of integration does an individual desire from the core of spiritualism? How should he orient himself from the behavioural points of view to achieve the best of spiritualism? All these and a host of other queries in connection with spiritualism do not skip the arena of Gandhian spiritualism. As a matter of fact, when Gandhi is concerned with his *Sarvodaya* which in the true sense of the term stands for the awakening of one and all, he essentially pays greater attention to the spiritual advancement of man from all possible directions than to anything else. This is primarily because Gandhi earnestly feels that any step towards advancement is a spiritual beginning – a beginning that is purely holistic and embraces all good sense and sensibilities of mankind. He, therefore, thinks that a human being is twice blessed with the essence of rationality and that of spiritualism. A synchronization of these two attributes for spiritual development by means of the principles of *Sarvodaya* is beyond the theory of Jeremy Bentham who believes in the greatest good of the greatest number, for Gandhi does not believe in this Benthamite doctrine. He rather considers it to be inadequate for human endeavour. This is evident from *The Diary of Mahadev Desai* where he explicitly remarks:

> I do not believe in the doctrine of the greatest good of the greatest number. It means in its nakedness that in order to achieve the supposed good of 51 per cent the interest of 49 per cent may be, or rather, should be sacrificed. It is a heartless doctrine and has done harm to humanity. The only real, dignified human doctrine is the greatest good of all, and this can only be achieved by uttermost self-sacrifice.
>
> – Valji Govindji Desai (Ed.): *The Diary of Mahadev Desai*, Navajivan Publishing House, 1953. Vol. II, p. 149.

The inherent spirit of *Sarvodaya* as "the greatest good of all" as Gandhi asserts is an earnest human endeavour for spiritual regeneration and, as such, it ensures a definite pattern of socio-political emancipation of man. He strongly feels that man must rise above utilitarianism that narrows down the all-embracing human spirit of sacrifice and boosts drab self-interest and self-satisfaction. On December 9, 1926, he observed:

> A votary of *ahimsa* cannot subscribe to the utilitarian formula (of the greatest good of the greatest number). He will strive for the greatest good of all and die in the attempt to realize the ideal. He will therefore be willing to die, so that the others may live. He will serve himself with the rest, by himself dying. The greatest good of all inevitably includes the good of the greatest number, and therefore, he and the utilitarian will converge in many points in their career but there does come a time when they must part company, and even mark in opposite directions. The utilitarian to be logical will never sacrifice himself. The absolutist will even sacrifice himself.
>
> – M.K. Gandhi: *Young India*, December 9, 1926.

The quintessence of Gandhi's *Sarvodaya* lies in the spiritual emancipation of man. Human welfare as he distinctly foresees, depends not on material progress but on spiritual advancement. Man, being man, cannot ignore his higher self, the self that leads him to spiritual poignance, and, as such, the immediate need for the modern world is to denounce economy devoid of human welfare and pave avenues for emancipation of spiritualism by means of exercise of eternal values of simplicity and austerity. Then, and then only, every one would be conscious of the dignity of man as man and the dream of Universal Dawn, *Sarvodaya*, will come to a reality. More greed for power as the modern world frantically aspires after, will certainly lead to utter disaster of humanism and all good sensibilities of mankind as Gandhi gravely points out, will be rampantly erased out from mankind with the destruction of individuality:

> I look upon an increase in the power of the state with the greatest fear because, while apparently doing good by minimizing exploitation, it does the greatest harm to mankind by destroying individuality which lies at the root of progress.
>
> – *The Modern Review*, Calcutta, October 1935.

Admittedly, Gandhi was greatly inspired by Ruskin's *Unto This Last* that denounces materialism and directly makes affluence responsible for humanistic and spiritual poverty. In his thesis on *Sarvodaya* he endeavours to bring about an all round transformation of humanism through transcendence towards spiritualism:

> Indeed Gandhi believed that everybody could do what he had done. 'You are as strong as you think you are', he would say, 'You are as strong as I am'. This faith in the ordinary man is what illumines the path for us in the future. For his message is to all of us, to each one of us; and its burden is that the common man can yet reassert his humanism if he has faith in his cause.
>
> Gandhi's conception of *sarvodaya* signifies the welfare and service of all. A good life for all and not just for the majority provides the test. In the society of Gandhi's dreams, the most needy will be provided for and none will be forgotten or allowed to feel lost, 'Unto this last': even the least will be cared for. This grand dream of emancipation of man had other facets also.

Ruskin's *Unto This Last*, which Gandhi read in 1904, denounced classical economists for not conceiving economics in terms of human welfare and accused industrialism for being responsible for intensifying poverty and injustice. These ideas found a ready response in Gandhi's mind. The ideal of a simple life and the stress of manual work took on their true significance in his quest. He found that though science and technology had given a new turn to the wheel of production and wealth, men were not only not emancipated, but were in fact being exploited. To Gandhi man himself was the cause of his own exploitation, because he had treated machines and a huge centralized structure and thus both in the political and economic fields, man had defeated man. He therefore, called for a review of the old assumptions and for a reassessment of the scale of values. His emphasis on simplicity and limitation of wants, his stress on decentralization and participation by the common man in the decision-making process at various levels, his call to men to work with joy, his emphasis on a united but not a uniform world – all this has current relevance.

– S. Chakravarti: "Truth and Non-violence in Gandhi's Humanism"
Quoted from *Truth and Nonviolence*, edited by
T.K. Mahadevan, Gandhi Peace Foundation,
New Delhi, 1970, pp. 39-40.

For a cohesion of consciousness and spiritualism, Gandhi takes recourse to *Sarvodaya* in which everyone undergoes an inner change both mentally and spiritually. He, therefore, gives importance to some of its strategic components as follows:

(i) *Nyaya* (Justice)
(ii) *Abhaya* (Fearlessness)
(iii) *Ahimsa* (Nonviolence)
(iv) *Brahmacharya* (Celebacy)
(v) *Sareer-srama* (Physical labour)
(vi) *Parartha-Bhavana* (Benevolence)
(vii) *Sparsa-Bhavana* (Sympathy)
(viii) *Sarvadharma-Samabhavana*
(Thoughts for Equality of all Religions)
(ix) *Satyagraha* (Truth-force)

Admittedly, Gandhi expands the horizon of the spiritual consciousness of humanity by launching his movement of *Sarvodaya*. The elevation of work to worship as a spiritual force enhances man's endeavour to himself by means of knowing others. This is what Gandhi terms as *Nyaya* or justice. This spiritual component of *Sarvodaya* allows every one to evaluate himself in terms of doing right under any trying circumstances. This also enables him to stick to justice that makes room for effulgence of heroism in the light of true erudition. He allows what is True, Good and Beautiful and rejects whatever stands in the way of the well-being of all. This is possible for him because the spiritual force of *Sarvodaya* also teaches and trains his mind how to win over all possible forms of cowardice. In fact, the spirit of *Sarvodaya* equips him with the spirit of *abhaya* that stands for fearlessness. As a spiritual component, fearlessness defends righteousness that comes out victorious in the long run. *Satyameva jayate* – Truth wins – is the spiritual foundation of *sarvodaya* that stands unvanquished against all evil forces. As the process is endless, Truth under the banner of *sarvodaya* embraces *ahimsa* or non-violence. Spiritually, *sarvodaya* unfolds *ahimsa* as a five-fold strategic force:

(a) As an introspective force, *ahimsa* prepares an individual to encounter his own limitations little or great and orients himself accordingly for the greater good of mankind.

(b) The inconsistencies and disparities between thought and action that appear in the behavioural designs of an individual are further checked and reconstructed, keeping in view the fact that Truth never dies and violence only begets violence.

(c) The spirit of non-violence is also the spirit of self-defence and as such, the components of self-defence cannot but nursle the virtues of the all-round welfare of all which is the core of *sarvodaya* as a spiritual force.

(d) The forces of violence are nothing but the forces of the inherent disintegrations of mankind. Integrate or perish is the introspective vision of *sarvodaya* which can be best exercised by following the principles of non-violence.

(e) *Ahimsa* as an antagonistic force against violence becomes more endearing to *sarvodaya* than anything else primarily because the latter never claims any endeavour as an end but only a means to one's spiritual excellence and poignance.

Bearing in mind the above strategic forces of *ahimsa* as an outcome of the spiritual efflorescence of *sarvodaya*, one might recall Gandhi's own interpretation of *ahimsa* that emerges as a great spiritual force of love for the awakening of all:

> If I am a follower of *ahimsa*, I *must love* my enemy. I must apply the same rules to the wrong-door who is my enemy or a stranger to me, as I would to my wrong doing father or son. This active *ahimsa* necessarily includes truth and fearlessness. As man cannot deceive the loved one, he does not fear or frighten him or her. Gift of life is the greatest of all gifts; a man who gives it in reality, disarms all hostility. He has paved the way for an honourable understanding. And none who is himself subject to fear can bestow that gift. He must therefore be himself fearless. A man cannot practise *ahimsa* and be a coward at the same time.
>
> – M.K. Gandhi: *Speeches and Writings of Mahatma Gandhi*, G.A. Natesan & Co., Madras, p. 346.

For an awakening of the greatest courage within oneself Gandhi appeals for the practice of *ahimsa* as a positive spiritual force – the force, that never knows how to yield towards selfishness and timidity. In fact, as a spiritual follower of *sarvodaya* what is of utmost importance is to look within, to purify within in order to best look outside and work steadfastly to the well-being of humanity. The self of the doer or worker in line with the spiritualistic vision of *sarvodaya* merges in the self of each and every person with whom he comes in contact directly or indirectly, and the resultant force of *ahimsa* as an obvious component of *sarvodaya* merges in the form of ever-mingling spirit of unison and harmony. Naturally, at such a stage of human consciousness, everyone is christened with the spirit of beyonding, that ever-glorious spirit which teachers him to cease to be within himself and spurn his little self to visualize face to face the God of Truth – *Satyanarayana*.

To visualize *Satyanarayana* in the spiritual mirror of *Sarvodaya* as Gandhi practically shows, is to be armed with the weapon of fearlessness – *abhaya* – that indicates true religion. 'The path of *Hari*' – the Lord of the light of spiritualism is the path of elimination of fear, for the latter is the destroyer of all spiritual accomplishments that *sarvodaya* fondles with all care and caution. And, in fact, it is the spiritual lesson of *sarvodaya* that primarily teaches everyone to be brave. In the words of Gandhi.

> Fearlessness is the first requisite of spirituality. Cowards can never be moral. Where there is fear there is no religion.
>
> Every reader of the Gita is aware that fearlessness heads the list of the Divine Attributes enumerated in the Sixteenth chapter. Whether this is due to the exigencies of metre or whether the pride of place has been deliberately yielded to fearlessness is more than I can say. In my opinion however, fearlessness fully deserves the first rank assigned to it there. Fearlessness is the *sine qua non* for the growth of the other noble qualities. How can one seek truth or cherish love without fearlessness? 'The path of Hari (The Lord) is the path of the brave, not of cowards'. The brave are those armed with fearlessness.
>
> – R.K. Prabhu & U.R. Rao (complied): *The Mind of Mahatma Gandhi*, Oxford University Press, London, 1945, p 91.

With the exercise of *Sarvodaya* as a spiritual force, Gandhi rightly thinks that one can realize the Supreme and be attuned to the highest forms of spiritualism only when he sticks to fearlessness at all costs. All delusions can, then, be eliminated for the mind becomes free from fear. This is all the more necessary as one of the fundamental strategies of *Sarvodaya* because its first and immediate necessity is to remove external fear that is nourished by sensualities and physical attraction. Moreover, *sarvodaya* teaches the great lesson of self-sacrifice – the lesson to be brave enough to accept the challenge of accepting everyone as most endearing and forgetting about one's own being or becoming by translating the truth of the noble commandment *Tena tyaktena bhunjithah* into reality. This note of spiritualism in the Gandhian philosophy of *Sarvodaya* is characteristically revealed as follows:

> Perfect fearlessness can be attained only by him who has realized the Supreme, as it implies the height of freedom from delusions. But one can always progress towards this goal by determined and constant endeavour. As for the internal foes, we must ever walk in their fear. We are rightly afraid of animal passion, anger and the like. External fears cease of their own accord, when once we have

conquered these traitors within the camp. All fears revolve round the body as the centre and would therefore disappear as soon as one got rid of the attachment for the body. Fear has no place in our hearts when we have shaken off the attachment for wealth, for family and for the body. '*Tena tyaktena bhunjithah*' is a noble commandment. The wealth, the family and the body will be there, just the same; we have only to change our attitude to them. All these are not ours, but God's. Nothing whatever in this world is ours. Even we ourselves are His. The *Upanishads* therefore direct us to give up attachment for things.

– *Ibid.*, pp. 91-92.

The fusion of interest of the individual self with that of the greater self, the Supreme is at the core of Gandhian spiritualism and *sarvodaya* is a vehicle of the efflorescence of that form of spiritualism. But, then, Gandhi emphasizes on a very important aspect of human endeavour – the endeavour to prepare oneself for attainment of spiritual excellence by means of conforming to *Brahmacharya* which is a continual process of mental and spiritual purification. The appalling ignorance of passion and sensualism, the moratorium of consciousness and aversion to simplicity and integrity sordidly contribute to the devaluation of human values. Under such circumstances, every person has no way out but to become a prey to sensuality and sentimentalism, greed and vandalism which tarnish every possibility of knowing himself and making himself worthy of the essential spiritual qualities lying dormant in him.

In fact, when Gandhi speaks of *Brahmacharya* as a great spiritual force for inner awakening he nursles his spiritual vision in the light of *sarvodaya*. The very ideal of *Brahmacharya* breaks the narrow barriers of religion and conservatism. Furthermore, it breaks the walls of isolation between man and man. It serves as a strategy of newer awakening of mankind to eliminate the narrow meaning of control of passions specially physical. Gandhi, indeed, reminds us of the actual meaning of *Brahmacharya* which, in his own words, stands for 'the conduct which puts one in touch with God'. Man, thus oriented in the spiritual concept of *sarvodaya*, prepares himself to be in unison with the All Beautiful. As he characteristically observes on the role of a person in pursuit of *Brahmacharya*:

The conduct consists in the fullest control over the senses. This is the true and relevant meaning of the word.

Popularly it has come to mean mere physical control over the organ of generation. This narrow meaning has debased *brahmacharya* and made its practice all but impossible. Control over the organ of generation is impossible without proper control over all the senses. They are all inter-dependent. Mind on the lower plane is included in the senses. Without control over the mind mere physical control, even if it can be attained for a time, is of little or no use.

– M.K. Gandhi: *Harijan*, June 13, 1936.

Perhaps Gandhiji in analysing and appreciating *Brahmacharya* as an invaluable spiritual component of *sarvodaya* is hallowed by the light of *Brahma* which stands for the *Atman* that proclaims the glory of man. And the *Atman* nowhere else dwells better than in the heart, the luminous spiritual city of man. Let every *Brahmachari* be an eternal follower of the spiritual light that awaits the luminous glow of perfection. Let all souls be in march for that spiritual awakening and advancement by which the unison with the *Manomayah*, the Great Mingler within the mind of all is possible. As the *Mundaka Upanishad* muses on:

Yah sarvajnah sarvavit yasyaisa mahima bhuvi;
divye Brahmapure hyasa vyamni atma pratisthitah
Manomayah pranasariraneta pratisthite'nne hrdayam sannidhaya
tat vijnanena paripasyanti dhirah anandarupam amrtam yat vibhati –

– *Mundaka Upanisad* (II. ii. 7-8)

['He whose glory is (seen) in the universe, who knows everything, who understands everything – He, this Atman, is established in the luminous space of the city of *Brahman* (the heart). He assumes forms of the mind, and leads the senses and the body. He dwells in the body, inside the heart. The wise ones, through realization, see Him everywhere – the one that shines in the world as the blissful and the immortal.']

In following *Brahmacharya* what Gandhi wants everyone to be a partner to the blessings of the All Luminous is to cultivate the spiritual essence of *sarvodaya* in the form of ' a constant endeavour to bring the mind under control'. For such an awakening of the mind, the first and foremost duty of every individual is to guard himself all the time against all evils and imperfections in 'thought, word and deed'. That is the most successful spiritual endeavour of mankind. In his own words, Gandhi explains the real significance of *Brahmacharya* as follows:

> *Brahmacharya* must be observed in thought, word and deed. It may be harmful to suppress the body, if the mind is at the same time allowed to go astray. Where the mind wanders, the body must follow sooner or later.
>
> It is necessary here to appreciate a distinction. It is one thing to allow the mind to harbour impure thoughts; it is a different thing altogether if it strays among them in spite of ourselves. Victory will be ours in the end, if we non-co-operate with the mind in its evil wanderings.
>
> We experience every moment of our lives, that often while the body is subject to our control, the mind is not. This physical control should never be relaxed, and in addition we must put forth a constant endeavour to bring the mind under control.
>
> – M. K. Gandhi: *From Yeravda Mandir, op. cit.*, p. 18

For a real follower of *sarvodaya*, the spiritualistic vision of *sarvamangalabhavana* – the thought of doing good to all mankind – becomes a reality, a *brata*, a pursuit to be strictly and sincerely adhered to under any circumstances. Constraints are there in legion. But *sarvodaya* as a spiritual force allows and equips everyone to be valiant enough to fight against all oddities and proclaim the victory of Truth everytime and everywhere. The preparation for having such a spiritual vision as *sarvodaya* is effulged within, is, of course, strenuous and unending. But, then, the pleasure of such a spiritual force as *sarvodaya* within an individual is also unending and therefore, incomparable. It is a pleasure of the mind, undefinable, irresistible, stimulating, pulsating, and, above all, everlasting.

In fact, like a true *yogi* – the spiritual ascetic – Gandhi wants efflorescence of pure spiritual consciousness through *sarvodaya* so that everyone might be free from all desires. Such a person being free from all desires, can dedicate himself wholeheartedly to the all round well-being of humanity. This is nothing but meditation for the highest spiritual endeavour leading to consciousness pure and infinite, which is certainly backed by the Indian spiritual line of thinking as revealed in the *Gita*:

> *Yada viniyatam cittam*
> *atmanyevavavisthate*
> *Nihsprhah sarvakamebhyo*
> *Yukta ityucyate tada.*
>
> — *Gita*, VI. 18

['When the completely disciplined mind rests in the Atman alone, free from longing after all desires, then is one called steadfast in *yoga*'.]

> *Yatha dipo nivatastho*
> *nengate sopama smrta*
> *yogino yatacittasya*
> *yunjato yogamatmanah* –
>
> — *Gita*, VI. 19

['As a lamp sheltered from wind does not flicker, even so is the smile for a *yogi* of disciplined mind practicing concentration of the Atman.']

Admittedly, a sincere follower of *sarvodaya* cannot but enjoy the thrilling spiritual experience of a *yogi* striving for greater and more disciplined spiritual perfection. At such a state of mind the spiritual joy is derived from the awakening of the sarvodayic sense of *parartha-bhavana* – the thought of doing good to others exercising both intrinsically and extrinsically extinction of personality.

It might be erroneously misapprehended that to exercise such as extinction of personality as stated above is possible only for a person of great spiritual attainment like Gandhi himself. But Gandhi, in fact, never claims himself to be either an ascetic or a *yogi*, a spiritual leader but an ordinary man like us who always ignores isolation from the millions of toiling masses. Furthermore, his movement with the spirit of non-violence is rooted in the heart of humanity. As a truth-force, non-violence serves as an introspective spiritual force of *parartha-bhavana* that highlights *sarvodaya* in the most desirable and natural form of manifestation. Gandhi's own interpretation on his own spiritual evolution as an exponent of *sarvodaya* deserves reference:

> It is wrong to call me an ascetic. The ideals that regulate my life are presented for acceptance by mankind in general. I have arrived at them by gradual evolution. Every step was thought out, well considered, and taken with the greatest deliberation. Both my continence and non-violence were derived from personal experience and became necessary in response to the calls of public duty. The isolated life I had to lead in South Africa whether as a householder, legal practitioner, social reformer or politician, required, for the due fulfilment of these duties, the strictest regulation of sexual life and a rigid practice of non-violence and truth in human relations, whether with my own countrymen or with the Europeans. I claim to be no more than an average man with less than average ability. Nor can I claim any special merit for such non-violence or continence as I have been able to reach with laborious research. I have not the shadow of doubt that any man or woman can achieve what I have, if he or she would make the same effect and cultivate the same hope and faith.
>
> – M.K. Gandhi: *Harijan*, October 3, 1936.

With such a spiritual endeavour as a follower of *sarvodaya*, Gandhi makes his sound platform on the realistic elements of life and thrusts himself wholeheartedly towards the welfare of humanity. This involvement has definitely been backed by the Upanishadic theory of endearment of the world as a joyous partner of mankind. When a person is spiritually enlightened he actually feels that he is identical with the joys and pleasures of the world whereby the fusion between him and the All Beautiful who is full of joy and pleasure, becomes a reality. He also feels that everything is full of joy because everything is the creation of the All Joyful. As the *Upanishad* says:

Iong prithivi sarvesang bhutanang
Madvasyai prithvyai sarvani bhutani
Madhu yaschayamasyang prithivyang
Tejomayohamritamayah purusho yaschayamadhyatmang
Sarirastejomoyohamritamayah purusohayameta
Sa johayamatmedamritamidang brahmedang sarvam.

– *Vrihadaranyak Upanishad*: 2:5:1

To a follower of the spiritual force of *sarvodaya* the world becomes akin to himself – the world that is both diverse and pleasant. The fulness of joy as a spiritual outcome of *sarvodaya* finds its brilliance of lustre in the canvas of a mind that humbly submits to the All Joyful. Why does Gandhi nursle such a spiritual vision in the light of *sarvodaya*? Perhaps the wants everyone to be a spiritual partner to the All Joyful. Perhaps he wants to be spiritually guided by Him who is the 'King of kings', in the same fashion as Tagore does:

> Thus it is that thy joy in me is so full. Thus it is that thou hast come down to me. O thou lord of all heavens, where should be thy love if I were not?
>
> Thou hast taken me as thy partner of all this wealth. In my heart is the endless play of thy delight. In my life thy will is ever taking shape.
>
> And for this thou who art the King of kings hast decked thyself in beauty to captivate my heart. And for this thy love loses itself in the love of thy lover, and there art thou seen in the perfect union of two.

– Rabindranath Tagore: *Song Offerings*, Macmillan Pocket Tagore Edition, Macmillan India Limited, New Delhi, 1983, No. 56, p. 37.

Again, the spiritual efflorescence of *sarvodaya* also shows the way of contentment in austerity. It is the inherent awakening of a person to be in continual pursuit of plenty in the midst of apparent poverty. It is an intrinsic spirit to harmonize all untoward forces that stand in the way of knowing the poignance of promise and perfection within himself. Gandhi himself maintains this spiritual awakening by means of simplicity and austerity in action and contemplation, behavioural design and manifestation. Who ignores the unique and unparalleled practice of spiritual entity through *sarvodaya* as he has done and maintained till the last breath of life by leading a very simple and austere life? His loin cloth is the eternal symbol of simplicity and austerity. His observance of daily life in the most ordinary and humble fashion, and never in extravagance and affluence, is the telling and living example of spiritualism practised in sincerity and devotion. As a matter of fact, when he speaks of the role of a *satyagrahi*, he maintains this view that his prime role as a follower of the principle of *sarvodaya* is to see that he remains humble and sincere all the time in plain living and spiritual thinking. His principle of humility is spiritual rather than being bare realistic for he adds the vision of *sarvodaya* to highlight the All Graceful who always tests mankind under trying circumstances. He therefore, looks upon the role of a *satyagrahi*, a messenger of the All Graceful, as a spiritual embodiment of *sarvodaya*. As he elucidates,

> The *satyagrahi*'s course is plain. He must stand unmoved in the midst of all cross currents. He may not be impatient with blind orthodoxy, nor be irritated over the unbelief of the suppressed people. He must know that his suffering will melt the stoniest heart of the stoniest fanatic and that it will also be a wall of protection for the wavering *Panchama* brother who has been held under suppression for ages. He must know that relief will come when there is least hope for it. For such is the way of the cruelly kind Deity who insists upon testing his devotee through a fiery furnace and delights in humbling him to the dust.
>
> – M.K. Gandhi: *Young India*, June 4, 1925.

With the spiritualistic force of *sarvodaya* in the form of non-violence, the sense of humility as Gandhi advocates, is internally strengthened in the form of the spirit of valour. The valiant in spirit is the worshipper of the awakening of good sense and sensibilities of one and all. He never cares for his loneliness nor does he feel insecure for being alone or single. The spirit that he cultivates within him always protects him from any insecurity whatsoever. How does this state of mind actually take place within an individual? How does he overcome the absence of being armed to retaliate against odds and evils? It is, as Gandhi strongly emphasizes, to take a firm resolution within to materialize in thought, word and deed to do good to others thereby doing good to the self. *Sarvodaya* as a spiritual force teaches how to be always on the guard against self-deception. In the words of Gandhi,

> The taking of a view does not mean that we are able to observe it completely from the very beginning; it does mean constant and honest effort in thought, word and deed with a view to its fulfilment. We must not practise self-deception by resorting to some make-believe.
>
> – M.K. Gandhi: *From Yeravda Mandir, op. cit.*, p. 25.

To take a vow in order to make a ceaseless and sincere endeavour in 'thought, word and deed' as Gandhi advocated, denotes the spiritual sense of self-development and self purification. And this spiritual sense allows an individual to be blessed with the divine grace that emanates from the spirit of *sarvodaya* in the form of self-surrender. This spiritual sense, again, promises an individual to be christened with the grandeur of 'be thou whole'. Perhaps Gandhi as an exponent of spiritualism in his theory and practice of *sarvodaya* comes closest to the message of Jesus:

> Come unto me, all ye that labour and are heavy laden, and I shall give you rest. Take my yoke upon you and learn of me, for I am meek and lonely in my heart; and ye shall find rest unto your souls. For my yoke is easy and my burden is light.
>
> – *St. Matthew*, 11. 28-30.

Perhaps again, Gandhi is foreoriented with the spiritual vision of the *Gita*:

> *Manmanā bhave madbhakto*
> *madyaji mām namaskuru;*
> *Māmevaisyasi satyam te*
> *prasijnane prio'se me* –
>
> – *Gita*, Ch. XVIII, 64 & 65.

[Absorb your mind with thought of Me, be My devotee, sacrifice unto Me, bow down to Me; truly do I promise you that you shall, verily reach Me, (for) you are dear to Me.]

With the spiritual awakening of man by means of following the Gandhian principle of *sarvodaya*, the inconsistencies and shortcomings of man are so eliminated as to make the fusion between the All Graceful and man a reality as it is clear from above that everyone is endearing to Him.

Admittedly, with *sarvodaya*, Gandhi exposes the dynamic force of spiritualism. He also extends this spiritual vision both in theory and in practice. And when he speaks of his *sarvodaya* as a dynamic force of spiritualism he holds the progress of spiritualism from moral points of view. This means that the vision of goodness is significant because it is guided by the great spiritual force that transcends bare reason and allows mankind to practise the spiritual vision within everyone by any means whatsoever. In his exposure on the spirit of mankind, Gandhi characteristically remarks:

> Spirit is that moral being which informs the human body and which is imperishable. Spiritual progress is that which promotes the realization of that imperishable essence. What retards the progress of my neighbour must retard mine. * *
>
> Spirit itself is capable of intellectual dissection only up to a point. It transcends reason, hence it is a matter of faith.
>
> – M.K. Gandhi: *Harijan*, March 11,1933.

The spiritual essence of *sarvodaya* as Gandhi advocates brings closest to the fact that true worship is the worship of humanity. And, for this end in view, man must uphold to man the spirit of purity of perfection. Then alone, the dream of a truly humanized and awakened society would be translated into reality. Then alone, all human endeavour to self-development and self-appreciation would visualize perfection and poignance. Gandhi, therefore, highlights *sarvodaya* as a great spiritual force for regeneration of humanity. It shows the future avenue of mankind towards glorification of the Spirit Eternal.

Perhaps, from the above points of view, Gandhi comes closer to

Sri Aurobindo who considers the religion of humanity to be nothing but a process of elimination of human egoism and establishment of all enduring altruism. The dignity of the human being awaits a reorientation through spiritualism for a humanized society. As Sri Aurobindo observes,

> A religion of humanity may be either intellectual, or else a spiritual aspiration, partly the sign, partly the cause of a change of soul in humanity. The intellectual religion of humanity already to a certain extent exists in the mind of a few. The fundamental idea is that mankind is the godhead to be worshipped, no other idol, neither the nation, the State, the family nor anything else, not even Science, ought to take its place. Man must be sacred to man regardless of all distinctions. And all this is not to be held as an abstract and pious sentiment, but given full and practical recognition in the person of men and nations and mankind.
>
> This religion of humanity has already exercised a great influence and accomplished many things which orthodox religion failed to do effectively. Moreover, this religion has faith in humanity and its earthly future, it has largely humanized society, given new conceptions of the dignity of the human being and opened new vistas of his education, self-development and potentiality.
>
> But still in order to accomplish all its future, it must entirely prevail over its principal enemy – human egoism, the egoism of the individual, the egoism of class and nation. These it may at present soften, modify, but not to give place to the love of mankind, not to recognize a real unity between man and man, the ideal which was first expressed some thousands of years ago in the ancient vedic hymn and must always remain the highest injunction of the spirit within us.

– Sri Aurobindo: *The Ideal of Human Unity*, (Abridged)
Sri Aurobindo Pathamandir, Calcutta,
1972, Chapter XXXIV, pp. 122-123.

Deeply influenced by the inherent spirit of the *Gita*, Gandhi formulates his spiritual vision of *sarvodaya* in the pursuit of *Brahma*, the Supreme and the Imperishable. The idea of humility in the term of *adhibhuta* or a perishable individual striving endlessly for steadfastness of *prana* or life-force and for dispelling the darkness of ignorance, as Gandhi introspects, is born of the spiritual end in view derived from the voice of the Lord:

> Brahma is the imperishable Supreme aspect of God, and *adhyatma* is the individual soul living in the body of all beings as the doer and the enjoyer. Karma is the process through which all beings come into existence, or in other words the process of creation. *Adhibhuta* is myself as the perishable body, and *adhiyajna* is the individual soul purified through sacrifice.
>
> Thus whether as the body or as the foolish soul or as the purified soul or as Brahma, it is I who am everywhere. And never doubt this that he who meditates on Me in all these aspects at the hour of death, forgets himself, is careful of nothing and desirous of nothing will be united with Me. Whatever a man constantly dwells on in his mind and remembers at the time of death is realized by him. Therefore, at all times you should remember Me and set your mind and heart upon Me and you will surely come to Me. You may say that it is hard thus to stabilize the mind. But you take it from Me that one can become single-minded by daily practice and constant endeavour, for as I told you just now, all embodied beings are in the essence Myself in various forms. For this he should prepare himself from the very first so that his mind does not go astray at the time of death, but is steeped in devotion, keeps the life force (*prana*) steady, and thinks only of Me as the omniscient, the ancient, the ruler, the subtle supporter of all and dispeller of ignorance like the sun which derives darkness away.
>
> — M.K. Gandhi : *In Search of the Supreme* (Ed. by V.B. Kher), Navajivan Publishing House, Ahmedabad, 1962, Vol. III, pp. 249-250.

The perfection of life is the perfection of the spiritual vision of *sarvodaya* to strive hard and strive unendingly. For this, self-realization alone can eliminate imperfections and all human limitations. What is the best strategy for self-realization?

The spiritual lesson of *sarvodaya* in the form of exercise of perfect humility as Gandhi elucidates in connection with Truth provides us with the best way out, the best answer:

> What . . . is Truth? A difficult question; but I have solved it for myself by saying that it is what the voice within tells you. How then, you ask, different people think of different and contrary truths? Well, seeing that the human mind works through innumerable media and that the evolution of the human mind is not the same for all it follows that what may be truth for one may be untruth for another, and hence who have made these experiments have come to the conclusion that there are certain conditions to be observed in making those experiments . . . . It is because we have at the present moment everybody claiming the right of conscience without going through any discipline whatsoever that there is so much untruth being delivered to a bewildered world. All that I can in true humility present to you is that truth is not to be found by anybody who has not got an abundant sense of humility. It you would swim on the bosom of the ocean of Truth you must reduce yourself to a zero.
>
> – R.K. Prabu & U.R. Rao: *op. cit.,* p. 17.

It is interesting to note in this connection that when Sri Aurobindo speaks on the spiritual religion of humanity, he also highlights the inner Truth as the eternally growing spirit of humanity – the sense of oneness of mankind striving for the kingdom of the 'divine spirit upon earth'. It also echoes the truth of the spiritual vision of *Sarvodaya* as Gandhi highlights. The onward march of Truth in an individual for the welfare of humanity is the core of *sarvodaya* which in Sri Aurobindo's vision of the higher aspirations of humanity finds revelation as follows:

> A spiritual religion of humanity is the hope of the future. By this we do not mean what is ordinarily called a universal religion, a system, a thing of creed and intellectual belief. Mankind has tried unity by that means; it has failed and deserved to fail. What is meant is the growing realization that there is a secret Spirit, a divine reality, in which we are all one and of which humanity is the highest vehicle on earth and that the human race and the human being are the means by which it will progressively reveal itself here, with a growing attempt to live out this knowledge and bring about a kingdom of this divine spirit upon earth. To go into all that this implies would be too large a subject to be entered

> upon here; it is enough to point out that in this direction lies eventual road. No doubt, if this is an idea like the rest, it will go the way of all ideas; but if it is at all a truth of our being, then it must be the truth to which all is moving and in it must be found the means of a fundamental, an inner, complete, a real human unity which would be the one secure basis of a unification of human life.
>
> – Sri Aurobindo: *The Ideal of Human Unity* (Abridged Ed.) Aurobindo Pathamandir, Calcutta, 1972, pp. 127-128.

In *Sarvodaya*, Gandhi upholds that form of spiritualism which fosters religion with the spirit of evolution. Man excels and exceeds himself not merely because he is a man, a bare rational being but essentially because he can exceed himself, make a real revolution within himself and disseminate the truth of *sarvamangala-bhavana* – the thought of the good of all – everywhere. In fact, 'an inner, a complex, a real human unity' as Sri Aurobindo visualized, finds the active, pulsating and poignant spiritual form of revelation in Gandhi's *sarvodaya*.

Admittedly Gandhian spiritualism finds an unparalleled form of revelation in *Sarvodaya* that has given an altogether new, practical, dynamic and living concept of God. An inherent 'marvellous force' as *sarvodaya* is, it highlights a better, continually improving and improvised behavioural pattern of manifestation of every human being. This is justified in his explanation of *Ramanama* at a prayer discourse:

> "Am I propagating a new variety of superstition?" asked Gandhiji in the course of one of his recent prayer discourses at Poona. "God is not a person. He is the all-pervading, all-powerful spirit. Anyone who bears Him in his heart has accession of a marvellous force of energy comparable in its results to physical forces like steam or electricity, but much more subtle". *Ramanama* was not like black magic. It had to be taken with all that it symbolized. He likened it to a mathematical formula which sums up in brief the results of endless research and experimentation. Mere mechanical repetition of *Ramanama* could not give strength. For that, one had to understand and live up to the conditions attaching to its recitation. To take God's name one must lead a Godly life.
>
> – Pyarelal: "Weekly Letter", *Harijan*, July 14, 1946.

To lead 'a Godly life' as Gandhi makes it obligatory for every human being proves the point that he emphasizes more on spiritualism than on anything else and this is what *sarvodaya* always upholds. A broader approach to religion cannot but harmonize all spiritual aspects of human endeavour and for this Gandhi advocates a purity of vision in prayer through a spiritual approach ably guided by the principles of *sarvodaya*. In this connection one might recall his spiritual exposure on *Ramanama* that totally leaves aside religious conservatism and brings forth the core of *sarvodaya* in the form of the vision of God as an all-pervasive altruistic force:

> I must repeat for the thousandth time that *Ramanama* is one of the many names for God. The same prayer meetings have recitation from the Koran and Zend Avesta. Devout Muslims, for the very reason that they are devout, have never objected to the chant of *Ramanama. Ramanama* is not an idle chant. It is conceived as a mode of addressing the all-pervasive God known to me, as to millions of Hindus, by the familiar name of *Ramanama*. *'Nama'* at the end of *Rama* is the most significant part. It means the *'Nama'* without the *Rama* of history. Be that as it may, why should an open profession by me of my faith offend anybody, much less the Muslim League? No one is obliged to join these meetings and, having joined, is not obliged to take part in this chant. All that the visitors are expected to do is not to mar the harmony of the meeting and to tolerate the proceedings even when they are not in sympathy with any part.
>
> – M.K. Gandhi: *Harijan*, August 18, 1946.

Since Gandhi believes in freedom of ideas and sentiments ably guided by the spiritual vision of *Sarvodaya* he categorically remarks that in the name of spiritualism there is no room for theocracy. Admittedly, this is further explained in his concept of *'Ramarajya'* which has nothing to do with religious conservatism or hypocrisy. As Gandhi observes,

> As to the use of the phrase *'Ramarajya'*, why should it offend after my having defined the meaning many times? It is a convenient and expressive phrase, the meaning of which no alternative can so

> fully express to millions. When I visit the Frontier Province or address predominantly Muslim audiences I would express my meaning to them by calling it *Khudai Raj*, while to a Christian audience I would describe it as the kingdom of God on earth. Any other mode would, for me, be self-suppression and hypocrisy.
>
> –*Ibid.*

The nursling of spiritualism in the true sense of the term as Gandhi highlights by means of his principles of *Sarvodaya* is, therefore, based on a sound principle of morality and discipline. It also ensures extension of the superior course of action through contemplation and self-surrender. That every one of us needs a re-discovery of the little 'I' that continually stands in the way of emancipation of the greater 'I' that ultimately merges in the Greatest 'We', the emblem of the Spirit Eternal is the most significant lesson that can be had from *sarvodaya*. It heightens us to think and re-think not merely over ourselves, our little acts and vision alone, but essentially to think beyond which means to think over the beyonding of ourselves. This is perhaps the greatest gift of Gandhian spiritualism that has its sustenance from *sarvodaya*. It glorifies human reason and erudition from the essence of purity and restrains humanity from being an easy victim to sensalism and sentimentalism. As a matter of fact, Gandhi wants to uphold spiritualism through *sarvodaya* with all the efflorescence of delight derived from *buddhi* or reason that allows and thrives steadiness of mind and character. Undoubtedly, Gandhi is guided by the spiritual teaching of the Gita which also sings the glory of *buddhi* in the same vein as follows:

> 'Giving up attachment, and equal-minded in success and failure do all actions, O Arjuna established in the *yoga* (of *buddhi*); this evenmindedness is *yoga*!
>
> 'Action (prompted by sense-attraction and blind impulses) is far inferior, O Arjuna, to action guided by the *yoga* of *buddhi*; seek refuge in *buddhi*; small-minded are they who act for selfish advantage.'
>
> 'Endowed with *buddhi*, man goes beyond (the relativity of) both merit and demerit in this very life; strive, therefore, to acquire the *yoga* (of *buddhi*); *yoga* is skill in action'.
>
> 'The wise ones endowed with (the yoga of) *buddhi*, renouncing the fruits of action, freed for ever from the bondages of existence,

attain to that state which is beyond all evil'.

– The *Gita*, Chapter II, lines 48-51. Quoted from *Eternal Values For a Changing Society*, by Swami Ranganathananda, Bharatiya Vidya Bhavan, Bombay, 1984, Vol. I, Chapter II. p. 139.

Reason purified in the fire of the spiritual vision of *sarvodaya* as Gandhi advocated, allows an individual to look within for a humble submission to the All Serene. It is a preparation, a pledge to make a unison of reason and the inherent voice of awakening of the self. It is also a voice within that proclaims for self-preparation to have a sounder faith in the liberation of all pettiness and fear, obstacles and constraints. Perhaps Gandhi has the same spiritual vision of *sarvodaya* in the manner of conflict as Tagore transcends:

> Obstinate are the trammels, but my heart aches when I try to break them. Freedom is all I want, but to hope for it I feel ashamed.
>
> I am certain that priceless wealth is in thee, and that thou art my best friend, but I have not the heart to sweep away the tinsel that fills my room.
>
> The shroud that covers me is a shroud of dust and death; I hate it, yet hug it in love.
>
> My debts are large, my failures great, my shame secret and heavy; yet when I come to ask for my good, I quake in fear lest my prayer be granted.

– Rabindranath Tagore: *Gitanjali*, Macmillan India Limited, Macmillan Pocket Tagore Edition, 1981. No. 28, pp. 16-17.

Do we listen to the voice within for a beyonding of ourselves?

4

THE AESTHETICS OF GANDHIAN SPIRITUALISM

The mind of an individual is the temple of inner awakening. It is the source point of spiritual excellence. It creates and recreates an individual both internally and externally. Man is reborn with the mind reawakened and rejuvenated. For Gandhi, spiritualism is never a surprise but a serenity of mind, a preparation through unending practice for perfection in all directions by means of which one is blessed with *sthitadhi*, a state of perfect balance of mind to be truly spiritual. At such a stage of mind, one ignores fear, fame or foe, death, destruction or disappointment. At such a stage of mind, again, one is above defeat or dispossession, for the God of Truth whom Gandhi hails as *Satyanarayana,* visualises within. The inherent aesthetics of spiritualism prepares him to be aware of the fear of his own internal shortcomings to be eliminated before long by means of humility. As he characteristically remarks,

> We must give up all external fears. But the internal foes we must always fear. We are rightly afraid of animal passion, anger, and the like. External fears cease of their own accord, when once we have conquered these traitors within the camp. All such fears revolve round the body as the centre, and will, therefore, disappear as soon as one gets rid of attachment for the body. We thus find that all external fear is the baseless fabric of our own vision. Fear has no place in our hearts, when we have shaken off the attachment for wealth, for family and for the body. Nothing whatever in the world is ours. Even we ourselves are His. When we cease to be masters, and reduce ourselves to the rank of servants, humbler than the very dust under our feet, all fears will roll away like mist; we shall attain ineffable peace, and see *Satyanarayana* (the God of Truth) face to face.
>
> — M.K. Gandhi : *From Yeravda Mandir,* Navajivan Press, Ahmedabad, 1935, p. 43.

How to be justified within oneself in the pursuit of spiritualism? How to regularly regulate oneself in thought and action so that the aesthetics of spiritual endeavour finds the best possible avenue of efflorescence? For Gandhi, it is transcendence from imperfection to perfection, from conflict to 'calmness of mind, all passion spent' and from vicissitudes to clarity and poignance of vision. He, therefore, believes that Truth as a definite aesthetic component of spiritualism elevates the self, the All Serene. It is Truth, again, that shows the individual to win over his pitfalls gradually but convincingly. The triumph of Truth is the triumph of spiritualism, for the triumph of Truth stands for the true aesthetic adventure for fulness and perfection. It is something that definitely acts as a transcendental force from aesthetics to spiritualism. Gandhi therefore, looks upon art not an end in itself but a means to an end—an inward spiritual awakening a beauty born with all aroma and efflorescence of the inner self. Truth, therefore, is a beauty in the cocoon of spiritual grandeur — 'a right perception' as he poignantly asserts. In his own words,

> There are two aspects of things — the outward and the inward. It is purely a matter of emphasis with me. The outward has no meaning except in so far as it helps the inward. All true art is thus the expression of the soul. The outward forms have value only in so far as they are the expression of the inner spirit in man. Art of that nature has the greatest possible appeal for me. But I know that many call themselves artists, and we recognized as such, and yet in their works there is absolutely no trace of the soul's upward urge and unrest.
>
> All true art must help the soul to realise the inner self. In my own case, I find that I can do entirely without external forms in my soul's realization. My room may have blank walls; and I may even dispense with the roof, so that I may gaze out upon the starry heavens overhead that stretch in an unending expanse of beauty. What conscious art of man can give me the panoramic scenes that open out before me, when I look up to the sky above with all its shining stars? This, however, does not mean that I refuse to accept the value of productions of art, generally accepted as such, but only that I personally feel how inadequate these are compared with the eternal symbols of beauty in Nature. These productions of man's art have their value only so far as they help the soul onward towards self-realization.

> All truths, not merely true ideas, but truthful faces, truthful pictures, or songs, are highly beautiful. People generally fail to see beauty in truth, the ordinary man runs away from it and becomes blind to the beauty in it. Whenever men begin to see beauty in truth, then true art will arise.
>
> Truly beautiful creations come when right perception is at work. If these moments are rare in life, they are also rare in art.
>
> – M.K. Gandhi : *Young India,* November 13, 1924.

The inherent spirit of beauty as an outcome of Truth as Gandhi asserts through aesthetic experimentation paves a newer avenue of spiritual poignance. It is that spiritual poignance which is soaked in the aesthetics of humility. Fundamentally, Gandhi heavily banks upon the age-old Indian aesthetic tradition of spiritual involvement in being humble and devoted to exercise individuality in the process of continuity of culture and tradition, spiritualism and devotion. As a consequence, in his approach to spiritualism, the aesthetic components of humility and devotion never fall short of his benign endeavour at spiritual evolution. He, therefore, remains a carefree, ordinary, humble seeker of Truth, Beauty and Goodness that highlight his spiritual revolution. That he never claims any originality in his aesthetic approach to spiritual consciousness is further revealed from the fact that in spite of being a radical revolutionary, he never claims himself as a spiritual pathfinder. As Acharya J.B. Kripalani observes,

> Gandhiji's thoughts and ideas are new and revolutionary; yet he claims no originality for them. He often asserts that in his ideas he merely follows in the foot-steps of the old and is offering nothing new to the world. This was not said merely from modesty. Gandhiji in disclaiming originality is only working in consonance with the genius of his people. The great men of India have rarely claimed originality for themselves. All their thinking they held could be traced back to the old, time-honoured and recognised authorities. Often, the very names of those who thus introduced new ideas are not known. The new ideas are supposed to have been handed down from antiquity. The Indian genius has generally worked impersonally and anonymously. Whatever the originality of the conception and the contribution, it is racial and not individual. Even in the aesthetic field the artist was supposed

to work within the limit of long-established and recognised techniques and traditions. The most remarkable thing is that even so he could create new terms of beauty that were 'joy for ever'. This conformity, however, is more apparent than real. Today one can trace in Indian thought the progress of ideas through the ages. Only new thought and forms were subtly introduced under the guise of interpretation and commentary. The most original and revolutionary thinkers considered themselves as mere commentators, carrying on the old traditions and maintaining an unbroken continuity. Every thought and institution according to them was *Puratan* and *Sanatan,* old and eternal.

— Acharya J.B. Kripalani : "An Integral Approach to Gandhian Thought", *The Visva-Bharati Quarterly,* Visva-Bharati, Santiniketan, Gandhi Number, Vol. 35, Nos. 1-4 combined, May 1969 — April 1970, p. 206.

The aesthetics of Gandhian spiritualism has, therefore, its unevenness not in non-conformism but in traditionalism which, of course, has been crystallized in the thoughts and experiments that were conducted in the ordinary approach to life. Here is a spiritual thinker, who highlights spiritualism in a creative and innovative mind of his own that aesthetically moulds ideas anew and in a revolutionary fashion.[1] The path that Gandhi follows in spiritual endeavour is always guided by a certain aesthetic sense of simplicity and of controlled capacity. This is evident when he expounds and interprets the *Gita* in his own unassuming fashion and in the common tongue to prove how aesthetically unadorned the language of explanation might be at spiritual endeavour. Gandhi, therefore, stands out characteristically novel even in his effort at following the old thinkers and spiritual leaders. As Kripalani observes,

Gandhiji follows in the footsteps of the old masters and reformers. He does not rely upon elaborate arguments. He rarely quotes authorities. He had made no special or systematic study of the many subjects he dealt with. His studies were of a general character. He had made some study of religious literature but with the object of regulating his conduct as a responsible member of society and thereby of finding the truth or as much of it as was vouchsafed to a mortal necessarily with limited capacity. This did not always call for logical consistency. Gandhiji has written a commentary on the GITA. But he has made no references to the authority of the other scriptures or to earlier or contemporary commentators. Though his interpretation of the scripture is unique in several respects he has not made any effort to refute the arguments of other writers of commentaries of the GITA. Though he does not quote authorities and has created quite a literature about his own thought and work he has been usually sparing of words. In spite of their volume his writings are characterised by terseness and brevity. There is no superfluity of words. There is no effort at literary flourishes. Though unadorned, his style has a natural beauty of its own. He puts his ideas in the most simple annd easily understandable and yet telling language. He is so sparing of words that it may be said that he writes Sutras in the common tongue. These need elaboration, explanation and commentary.

— Acharya J.B. Kripalani : *Ibid.*, Vol. 35, Nos. 1, 2, 3 & 4, combined May 1960 — April 1970, p. 191.

Admittedly, even in spiritual endeavour at elucidating the poignant scriptures and *Sastras,* Gandhi remains true to the 'Kindred point of heaven and home'. The language is never lost in the labyrinth of ambiguities or complexities nor is there any slightest approach to exhibitionism as an iconoclastic authoritarian. This has brought forth an added fervour to his spiritual excellence — the fervour of inhaling the aesthetic fragrance of spiritualism. Thus when Gandhi speaks of Truth as a soul-force he combines the twofold aspect of aesthetics and spiritualism. Truth as an integral component of inner fulness heightens and broadens the soul. At the same time, the beauty of Truth expressed or manifested in terms of leading an ordinary, pure, humble and respectable life ennobles the inherent aesthetics and spiritualism of mankind.

Truly, Gandhi makes a classic connotation of Truth by allowing and accelerating in in terms of soul-force — a force that enables everyone to overcome the littleness and oddities of life. And, when he makes a fusion between aesthetics and spiritualism by means of sticktoitiveness to Truth, the search of the supreme becomes exceedingly fruitful. His ceaseless endeavour at understanding the truth of all religions is a beckoning of aesthetics that embraces spiritualism in religious faith. As he most humbly observes,

> I believe in the truth of all religions of the world. And since my youth upward, it has been a humble but persistent effort on my part to understand the truth of all the religions of the world, and adopt and assimilate in my own thought, word, and deed and all that I have found to be best in those religions. The faith that I profess not only permits me to do so but renders it obligatory for me to take the best from whatsoever source it may come.
>
> — M.K. Gandhi : *Harijan,* February 16, 1934.

With such a wide attitude towards embracing Truth from multi-dimensional source-points, Gandhi heightens spiritualism with the most benign aesthetic fervour thereby allowing humanism to be truly radical and revolutionary in approach and principle. In fact, a new aesthetic dimension of spiritualism is opened out in diverse religious principles when the truth of all religions is visualized by means of Gandhian aesthetic vision. The true brotherhood of man, then, will be a reality in all its aesthetic grandeur through a genuine understanding of global spiritual excellence. As Gandhi strongly asserts,

> I believe in the fundamental truth of all religions of the world. I believe that they are all God-given, and I believe that they were necessary for the people to whom these religions are revealed. And I believe that, if only we could all of us read the scriptures of different faiths from the standpoint of the followers of those faiths we should find that they were at bottom all one and were all helpful to one another.
>
> — M.K. Gandhi : *Harijan,* February 16, 1934.

A deep probe into the inner spiritual aspect of human faith as Gandhi has all the time made in conformity with aesthetic excellence is an altogether new and characteristic approach to spiritualism. As a matter of fact, he makes no compromise with narrowness of inward vision, for he has the clearest introspection that true spiritualism and true aesthetics are both one and the same. This means that when an individual makes a genuine spiritual endeavour, he cannot but embrace within himself all the components of aesthetic sensibilities.

Perhaps for this reason, if not for others as well, he values the aesthetic insight of Truth and Ahimsa as an integral part of self-confidence in spiritual endeavour. This is evident in his whole-hearted support for the Swaraj Party that would bring forth the desirable change of consciousness among the masses who would depend on Truth and *Ahimsa* both as a spiritual and as an aesthetic component of freedom of humanity. Being asked whether he is guilty of over-confidence, he categorically observes,

> I do not think so. For a man of truth must ever be confident if he has also equal need to be diffident. His devotion to truth demands the fullest confidence. His consciousness of the fallibility of human nature must make him humble and therefore ever ready to retrace his steps immediately he discovers his error. It makes no difference to his confidence that he has previously made Himalayan blunders. His confession and penance make him, if any thing, stronger for future action. Discovery of errors makes the votary of truth more cautious, of believing things and forming conclusions, but once he has made up his mind, his confidence must remain unshaken. His errors may result in men's reliance upon his judgements being shaken, but he must not doubt the truth of his position once he has come to a conclusion. It should further be borne in mind that my errors have been errors of calculation and judging men, not in appreciating the true nature of Truth and *Ahimsa* or in their application. Indeed, these errors and my prompt confessions have made me surer, if possible, of my insight into the implications of Truth and *Ahimsa*. For I am convinced that my action in suspending civil disobedience in Ahmedabad, Bombay and Bardoli has advanced the cause of India's freedom and world's peace. I am convinced that because of the suspensions we are nearer *Swaraj* than we would have been without, and this I say in spite of despair being written in thick black letters on the horizon. Such being my deep conviction, I cannot help being confident of my present position as regards Swarajists and other matters. It is traceable to one source only, a lively understanding of the implications of Truth and *Ahimsa*.
>
> — M.K. Gandhi : *Young India,* September 10, 1925.

The inherent aesthetics of Gandhian spiritual faith has its root in the insight of the unending strength of mankind. The heart that pulsates with such a spiritual insight as Gandhi time and again shows in contemplation as well as in action is always engineered with the true magic and miracle of aesthetic fulfilment. It is the aesthetic grandeur of spiritualism that embodies character-strength, service and love. It also endears other aesthetic components in one's spiritual insight such as peace, faith, fearlessness and dedication. Bereft of such aesthetic consciousness, one's spiritual excellence turns into nothingness, for one cannot avert the enemy within oneself — the enemy who tears apart by means of self-defeat and self-temptation. To conquer oneself, therefore, is the surest way to be hallowed with the aura of aesthetics in one's spiritual endeavour. Gandhi makes the fullest commitment to the teaching of the *Gita* in aiming at self-consciousness and self-discipline as aesthetic components of spiritual growth and fulfilment. And when, as he strongly advocates and himself strives for, one becomes one's own friend and is thus disciplined within oneself, one enjoys the blessings of spiritual perfection. Indeed, as an aesthetic spiritualist, he comes nearest to the teachings of the *Gita* in the *Dhyana Yoga*:

> *Bandhurātmātmanastasya*
> *Yenatmaivātmanā jitah;*
>
> *Anātmanastu Satrutva*
> *Vartetātmaiva satruvat*

– *Gita* (Ch. VI : Verse 6)

> [To conquer oneself is to become one's on friend; but when one fails to do so, one becomes, as it were, one's own enemy.]

The aesthetics of spiritualism as Gandhi exercises in his own life is never an end in itself, for in national life, too, in promoting tolerance, friendliness and, over and above, nationalism, he advocated faith and trust as a perennial spiritual force. As he observes,

> It matters little that one may have been deceived before or may have built hope on a proper foundation. Hope to be worth anything must 'spring eternal in the human breast'. Trust can have no limits. It must always give the benefit of the doubt. It is better to

> suffer a million disappointments than not to have trusted where mistrust was a mistake. A man who permits himself to be deceived is never the loser. Indeed, he is the gainer in the end, *not* the so-called successful deceiver. A thousand deceits would leave me unrepentant. My personal experience is that in spite of some very hard knocks which I can recall at the time of writing, I have no cause to regret the trustful nature with which the world around me has credited me. It is my conviction that I and those whom I have involved in my trustfulness have lost nothing, if we cannot prove to have always gained. A man loses only when he loses his soul and that can never be lost through another man's deceit.
>
> — M.K. Gandhi : *Young India,* November 22, 1928.

Truly, Gandhi exercises the aesthetics of mutual trust for spiritual efflorescence not because, the spirit of an individual would suffer but essentially because it shines amidst sufferings. In fact, his sense of faith in humanity is guided by the principles underlying the role of a *Sthitadhi* who remains undisturbed either in happiness or in sorrow, and who is above anger, fear or agitation — *Sukhesu anudvignamana duhkhesu vigataspriha/vitaraga-bhaya-krodha* — to achieve the aesthetic poignance of spiritualism. For this reason alone, Gandhi never loses faith in humanity. That human nature is not inelastic[2] heightens his firm spiritual faith and aesthetic vision of humanism. It has practically opened out a new dimension of aesthetic development in human behavioural design. An attitude of 'immutable faith' as he spiritually foresees can avert erosion of aesthetic sensibilities:

> My attitude towards the English is one of utter friendliness and respect. I claim to be their friend, because it is contrary to my nature to distrust a single human being or to believe that any nation on earth is incapable of redemption. * * * * A time is coming when England will be glad of Indian's friendship and India will disdain to reject the poffered hand because it has once despoiled her. I know that I have nothing to offer in proof of my hope. It is based on immutable faith. And it is a poor faith that is based on proof commonly so called.
>
> — M.K. Gandhi : *Young India,* January 29, 1925.

As an aesthetic spiritualist, Gandhi also eliminates the narrowness of mind nursed in debased suspicion of nature. While refuting the proposition that dependence on foreign dyes must be done away with in the manufacture of khadi because there is every possibility of betrayal from the ends of middlemen who would always harp on the discovery and use of native dyes, he observes.

> The Khadi movement stands for all-round purification. It requires us to establish contact with every sphere of social life and to exercise a purifying influence. We do not want to take away from the middleman his occupation, but only to give a new orientation to it and to change his mental outlook. We must have an abiding faith in the middlemen, and in their developing one day a high sense of business morality and a burning patriotism.
>
> — M.K. Gandhi : *Young India,* March 21, 1929.

To find out the best in man crystallized in both aesthetic and spiritual fulfilment is what Gandhi considers to be the most essential objective of the onward march for advancement of humanism. How does man equip himself with such an aesthetic and spiritual fulfilment? Gandhi has a definite answer that embraces all the characteristic aesthetic components of spiritualism. As a believer of *advaita* or oneness of man he simply believes that the spiritual and aesthetic enrichment of an individual actually denotes the excellence of all humanity. The whole world, then, enjoys the gifts of aesthetics as enkindled in the endeavour at spiritual excellence. As Gandhi humbly observes,

> I do not believe that an individual may gain spiritually and those that surround him suffer. I believe in *advaita.* I believe in the essential unity of man and for that matter of all that lives. Therefore I believe that if one man gains spiritually, the whole world gains with him, and if one man falls, the whole world falls to that extent.
>
> — M.K. Gandhi : *Young India,* December 4, 1924.

A rare aesthetic design of Gandhian spiritualism as set forth above in the altruistic approach to goodness of all mankind also highlights non-possession not as an ordinary act without an end in view but as an aesthetic practice of spiritual excellence. Such a practice is actually the practice of Truth that teaches the spiritual lesson of love towards all mankind. It is also the 'Divine Law' as Gandhi characterizes in terms of austerity. The aesthetic vision of the welfare of one and all is based upon this Divine Law which acts as a spiritual force in mankind. As a consequence, man cannot but think and act for the goodness of all. The appalling difference between the rich and the poor, the high and the low, the haves and the have-nots, the advantaged and the disadvantaged is eliminated in what Gandhi characteristically terms as 'a universal diffusion of the spirit of contentment' — an indomitable aesthetic force that controls the man squeezed and overpowered in material affluence and boosts the serene vision of altruistic spiritualism. The doctrine of Gandhian trusteeship, viewed in such an aesthetics of spiritualism, cannot but pave invaluable avenues of human excellence. As a matter of fact, Gandhi's own viewpoints serve a better exposition:

> Non-possession is allied to non-stealing. A thing not originally stolen must nevertheless be classified stolen properly, if one possesses it without needing it. Possession implies provision for the future. A seeker after Truth, a follower of Law of Love cannot hold anything against tomorrow. God never stores for the morrow; He never creates more than what is strictly needed for the moment. If, therefore, we repose faith in His providence, we should not rest assured, that He will give us everything that we require. Saints and devotees, who have lived in such faith, have always derived a justification for it from their experience. Our ignorance or negligence of the Divine Law, which gives to man from day to day his daily bread and no more, has given rise to inequalities with all the miseries attendant upon them. The rich have a superfluous store of things which they do not need, and which are therefore neglected and wasted, while millions are starved to death for want of sustenance. If each retained possession only of what he needed, no one would be in want, and all would live in contentment. As it is, the rich are discontented no less than the poor. The poor man would fain become a millionaire, and the millionaire a multi-millionaire. The rich should take the initiative in dispossession with a view to a universal diffusion of the spirit of contentment. If only they keep their own property within moderate limits, the starving will be easily fed, and will learn the

lesson of contentment along with the rich.

— M.K. Gandhi : *From Yeravda Mandir, op. cit.*, p. 34.

A sense of shamefulness arising out of the vain pride of demoralized humanity in self-deceit and absence of humility as an aesthetic component of spiritual grandeur always acts as a fillip to revolutionize mankind in spiritualism — in terms of self-esteem and naturalness in behavioural pattern. For this revolutionary aspect of Gandhi's personality, the spiritual appeal of *satyagraha* even now stands out as a supreme one for restoration of the aesthetic marvels of humanity.[3] Pride, then melts in the aesthetic fire of spiritual oneness of mankind. At the same time, the vision of the allround goodness of man in the light of living for the sake of others in order to live in the spiritual way directs mankind of the Gandhian aesthetics of *ahimsa*. Perhaps, the suggestion to voluntary starvation as a means to alleviate mass distress of poverty is an aesthetic approach to goodness to one and all. The underlying spirit of such an endeavour is to exercise spiritualism as a practical lesson in everyday affairs of life. Simplicity as a direct component of spirituality allows humanity to be wider in outlook and broader in the progressive march of mankind.

The inherent aesthetics of spiritualism as Gandhi maintains within himself, therefore, goes far beyond the domain of utilitarianism and allows the aesthetic spirit of altruism. His own exposition to this viewpoint serves better in understanding *ahimsa* as an aesthetic component of spiritualism:

> If I take anything that I do not need for my own immediate use, and keep it, I thieve it from somebody else. I venture to suggest that it is the fundamental law of Nature, without exception, that Nature produces enough for our wants from day to day, and if only everybody took enough for himself and nothing more, there would be no pauperism in this world, there would be no man dying of starvation in this world. But so long as we have got this inequality, so long we are thieving, I am no socialist and I do not want to dispossess those who have got possessions; but I do say that, personally those of us who want to see light out of darkness have to follow this rule. I do not want to dispossess anybody. I should then be departing from the rule of *ahimsa*. If somebody else possesses more than I do, let him. But so far as my own life

> has to be regulated, I do say that I dare not possess anything which I do not want. In India we have got three millions of people having to be satisfied with one meal a day, and that meal consisting of a *chapati* containing no fat in it, and a pinch of salt. You and I have no right to anything that we really have until these three millions are clothed and fed better. You and I, who ought to know better, must adjust our wants, and even undergo voluntary starvation in order that they may be nursed, fed and clothed.
>
> — M.K. Gandhi : *Speeches and Writings of Mahatma Gandhi,* G.A. Natesan & Co., Madras, p. 384.

Revamping socialism from the standpoint of the aesthetics of nobler living and greater feeling for the entire humanity is the essence of Gandhian spiritualism. As a human benefactor, Gandhi, therefore, places man as the votary of truth that unfolds that veil of ignorance to be hallowed with the spirit of light eternal. As he poignantly observes,

> I am more concerned in preventing the brutalization of human nature than in the prevention of the sufferings of my own people. I know that people who voluntarily undergo a course of suffering raise themselves and the whole of humanity; but I also know that people who become brutalized in their desperate efforts to get victory over their opponents or to exploit weaker nations or weaker men, not only drag down themselves but mankind also. And it cannot be a matter of pleasure to me or anyone else to see human nature dragged to the mire. If we are all sons of the same God and partake of the same divine essence, we must partake of the sin of every person whether he belongs to us or to another race.
>
> — M.K. Gandhi : *Young India,* October 29, 1931.

The Gandhian aesthetics of spiritual consciousness in the vision and realization of man as an inseparable part of God is yet to be translated in reality.

When will the entire humanity be christened with the spiritual choir of *Satyanarayana*?

NOTES

1. Acharya J.B. Kripalani makes the following characteristic observations:

   Whatever their external form of expression and presentation, Gandhiji's ideas are new and revolutionary. They arise out of the creative mind of an individual to whose reforming zeal the social situation and the difficulties of the times come as a challenge. For him historical precedents and examples are no barrier to fresh thinking and discovery. Gandhiji did not acquire his ideas and knowledge merely from books. He did not pass his time in libraries and museums pouring over musty volumes. Much of his knowledge was the result of direct contact with life and practical experiences it offers. He therefore placed his ideas before the public not in the language of the learned but of the average intelligent man of affairs. In explaining his ideas he does not use the philosophic and technical language of the schools. He was the man of the masses and spoke to them in their ordinary native dialect which they could understand. He addressed them not about what he had read and studied in books but what he had seen, sensed, experienced and thought about. He described his own observations and his reactions to them. This is the method that characterised great religious reformers and prophets. They were in touch with common humanity. Although his method is more suited to the intellectual capacity of the common man than the academic way, it readily appeals to him and carries conviction. However, oftentimes it leaves the intellectual and academic mind unconvinced and cold. Also Gandhiji was no great student of history. Like the prophets of old he created history. His practical schemes of work and explanations therefore created his philosophy.

   —Acharya, J.B. Kripalani : "An Integral Approach to Gandhian Thought", *The Visva-Bharati Quarterly,* Santiniketan, Gandhi Number, Vol. 35, Nos. 1, 2, 3 and 4, May 1969 — April 1970, pp. 188-189.

2. Gandhiji's explanation for his belief in the awakening of good sense and sensibilities among the British rulers of the-then India might be referred to as follows:

   I am made by nature to side with weak parties. My policy of non-embarrassment is based upon that nature and it persists. My proposal for British withdrawal is as much in the Britain's interest as India's. Your difficulty arises from your disinclination to believe that Britain can ever do justice voluntarily. My belief in the capacity of non-violence rejects the theory of permanent inelasticity of human nature.

   — M.K. Gandhi : *Harijan,* June 7, 1942.

3. Wolfenstein, in his significant study on why a man rebels, makes a comparative analysis of 'pride' as one of the characteristic traits of personality of Lenin, Trotsky and Gandhi as follows, where humility in case of Gandhi shines out most brilliantly as the best avenue of revolution both as an aesthetic and as a

spiritual force:

With respect of pride, and the self-assurance and naturalness of manner which results from it, Lenin ranks highest, Trotsky second and Gandhi last. Pride was not the major issue for Lenin at any discernable point in his adolescence or adult life. Trotsky worked out a solution to his feelings of shame fairly early, by his verbal humiliation of others, with the final pattern of conflict management not really set until he arrived in Europe and had more or less mastered Marxism. Gandhi was concerned with pride until his victory over humiliation in South Africa. His basic feelings of shamefulness, however, were so great that he had to allow himself to be humiliated, as he had to allow himself to suffer pain, in order to keep a reasonable harmony between his view of himself and what he perceived to be others' views of him. Both Trotsky and Gandhi had the good fortune to be living in times when a politicized solution to a personal problem of shame would have wide appeal. Unfortunately for both, but especially for Trotsky, each outlived the period of crisis which gave him power on the basis of that solution.

Because Trotsky and Gandhi or in more general terms the person troubled by shame, suffered from the consequences of ridicule and other unfavourable forms of attention, they had a residual fear of humiliation which inhibited their speaking and made them sensitive to insult, although Trotsky superbly overcame the former problem and Gandhi the latter. On the whole, however, the person lacking in basic pride or self-respect will be less able to bear acrimony, more likely to react by trying to humble the offender, than the person who is secure of his self-esteem. At the same-time, this person will crave attention and unless he can disguise his craving under an elaborate shield like Gandhi's assumed modesty, he will therefore be in danger of offending others by his apparent egotism and desire for applause. He probably will also have, however, the advantage of being more sensitive to the responsiveness of an audience than a less uncertain man, but here other variables, such as the person's capacity for empathy (which seems more likely to be an attribute of the self-respecting person) may tend to equalize the situation.

— Victor Wolfenstein : *The Revolutionary Personality : Lenin, Trotsky, Gandhi,* Princeton University Press, Princeton, New Jersey, 1967, pp. 162-163.

5

RELIGION AND SPIRITUALISM: The Gandhian Bonds of Harmony

The mind of man is never unholy. It is as all religion believes, the eternal temple of the Living God. It is a Temple of unending purified crystallized conscience. It is what the mind of man is — always striving for fullness of growth and development.

For Gandhi, the apostle eternal of spiritualism, the mind of man is something more. Since it is never unholy, the role of man to keep it always pure in thought and action, preparation and perfection never ceases. With limitations in legion of inconsistencies and imperfections, man strives hard to eliminate the shortcomings of his thoughts and deeds, and strive he must because he cannot but avert the call of conscience. As religion makes a living influence on the heart and life of man, Gandhi wants to make everyone aware of the fact that he has a definite role to bring about a change of consciousness, the birth of spiritualism, that upholds the real worth of man. Religion, then, gets the right perspective for efflorescence.

The ways and means of making bonds of harmony between religion and spiritualism in the history of human civilization are manifold and diverse. For Gandhi, the ways and means are always thrilling and penetrating. Since he maintains the view that his life is his message, he shows the bonds of harmony between religion and spiritualism in terms of real life situation which proves the Ruskinian truth that work is worship. Again, when he maintains the view that his God is represented in the bread of the poor, the lowliest and the lost, he accentuates the fact that service to man is service to God. The inner spirit of man is thus honoured and sanctified, and the bonds of harmony between religion and spiritualism are established in aesthetic fusion.

Apart from the fact that true religion is never a faith that appeals to the head alone but to the heart which should be purified and ennobled, Gandhi goes a step further in conceptualizing religion as an integral part of spiritualism that opens out newer dimensions of understanding and appreciating religion. How does he want to make a fusion? What are the fundamental principles of his theory of fusion between spiritualism and religion? What are the avenues of efflorescence that make religion and spiritualism identical and yet distinctive? What practical approaches and strategies can bring about a definite change of opinion in spiritualism and religion? These and a host of other enquiries related to the Gandhian concept of spiritualism and religion await learned attention and appropriate global exposition.

To realize the inner spirit of oneself, the spirit of conscience that appeals to the heart and not merely to the head or the intellect is the first lesson for man to prove his worth as man. And, for such a lesson to be learnt from day to day experience of life, man, as Gandhi strongly believes, must uphold his aesthetic sense for a purer vision and revelation of religion. Religion, then, shines out as a blooming flower of realization of the All Beautiful. A transformed and transcendental pattern of human behaviour backed by an introspective exercise of doing good to one and all as children of God is what goes beyond the luxuries of intellectual exercise to which modernity is exceedingly prone. As Gandhi elucidated,

> But He is no God who merely satisfies the intellect, if He ever does. God to be God must rule the heart and transform it. He must express Himself in ever the smallest act of His votary. This can only be done through a definite realization more real than the five senses can ever produce. Sense perceptions can be, often are, false and deceptive, however real they may appear to us. Where there is realization outside the senses it is infallible. It is proved not by extraneous evidence but in the transformed conduct and character of those who have felt the real presence of God within. Such testimony is to be found in the experience of an unbroken line of prophets and sages in all countries and climes. To reject this evidence is to deny oneself.
>
> — M.K. Gandhi : *Young India,* October, 11, 1928.

The bonds of harmony between spiritualism and religion are further strengthened by means of elimination of subjectivity. Then, for exercise of true religion as a true exponent of spiritualism, self-surrender and self-negation bring forth the desirable efflorescence of humility. Then, alone, the aura of true conscience shines in spiritual brilliance. Such an aura of conscience finds the Gandhian exposure as follows:

> Our existence as embodied beings is purely momentary; what are a hundred years in eternity? But if we shatter the chains of egotism, and melt into the ocean of humanity, we share its dignity. To feel that we are something is to set up a barrier between God and ourselves, to cease feeling that we are something is to become one with God. A drop in the ocean partakes of the greatness of its parent, although it is unconscious of it. But it is dried up as soon as it enters upon an existence independent of the ocean. We do not exaggerate, when we say that life is a mere bubble.
>
> A life of service must be one of humility. He, who could sacrifice his life for others, has hardly time to reserve for himself a place in the sun. * * * True humility means most strenuous and constant endeavour entirely directed towards the service of humanity.
>
> — M.K. Gandhi : *From Yeravda Mandir,* Navajivan Press, Ahmedabad, 1935, p. 68.

An abiding faith in the cohesion of human conscience in the patterns of humility and service on the one hand and surrender to the Living Law of the universe on the other synchronize spiritualism with religion. This, indeed, is the faith, living and dynamic, in the march of mankind that constitutes true religion. Gandhi's own experience is a pointer to the fact that such a faith is actually an obedience to the law of the universe. As he admits,

> My own experience has led me to the knowledge that the fullest life is impossible without an immovable belief in a Living Law in obedience to which the whole universe moves. A man without that faith is like a drop thrown out of the ocean bound to perish. Every drop in the ocean shares its majesty and has the honour of giving us the ozone of life.
>
> — M.K. Gandhi : *Harijan,* April 25, 1936.

The faith of life living and dynamic and soaked in 'the ozone of life' as Gandhi elucidates above makes inroads to religion through spiritualism which crystallizes and prepares the mind for better transcendence. The components of such transcendence are legion and therefore, direct humanity towards the holy grail. One of the components is the inner conscience which acts in the form of temper serves religion best for crystallization of behavioural design. In fact, the pursuit of all that is high and holy entirely depends on how one directs and redirects one's temper towards the holy and serene that represents true religion. What type of faith does Gandhi want to nurture in life? What are the Gandhian avenues of fusion between spiritualism and religion in terms of faith? The answer is, as Gandhi strongly believes and translates into action in real life situation, quite simple; it is to obey God in improvement of the inner self — the real self — that is pure, eternal, unvanquished and everlasting. It is also to improve humanity and dedicate oneself to benevolence to mankind. To love and obey God in the deepest inner faith of love and benevolence towards humanity is to exercise religion in the core of spiritualism. Gandhi looks upon faith not as an indistinct material force or merely a subjective outcome of mind but essentially a transcendental spiritual force that combines reason with realization of the All True and All Beautiful. That God is within every individual and is never an alien force or entity as one might visualize in vain is the most living and dynamic concept of religion. And this concept proves the point that there is a permanent bond between Good and religion that one enshrines within oneself in the forms of thinking, feeling, willing and, to be truly spiritual, being. Gandhi makes a characteristic analysis of religion reaching the full spiritual height :

> I know, too, that I shall never know God if I do not wrestle with and against evil even at the cost of life itself. I am fortified in he belief by my own humble and limited experience. The purer I try to become the nearer to God I feel myself to be. How much more should I be near to Him when my faith is not a mere apology, as it is today, but has become as immovable as the Himalayas and as white and bright as the snows on their peaks?

— R.K. Prabhu & U.R. Rao (Compiled) : *The Mind of Mahatma Gandhi,* Oxford University Press, London, 1945, p. 22.

Elsewhere, Gandhi poignantly observes,

> God has created different faiths just as He has the votaries thereof. How can I even secretly harbour the thought that my neighbour's faith is inferior to mine and wish that he should give up his faith and embrace mine? As a true and loyal friend, I can only wish and pray that he may live and grow perfect in his own faith. In God's house there are many mansions and they are equally holy.
>
> — M.K. Gandhi : *Harijan,* April 20, 1934.

With such a spiritual insight in religion Gandhi makes a deeper analysis of religion as based on the transcendence of reason. As he elucidates,

> Indeed, even the so-called realization has at bottom an element of faith without which it cannot be sustained. In the very nature of things it must be so. Who can transgress the limitations of his being? I hold that complete realization is impossible in the embodied life. Nor is it necessary. A living immovable faith is all that is required for reaching the full spiritual height attainable by human beings. God is not outside this earthy case of ours. Therefore, exterior proof is not of much avail, if any at all. We must even fail to perceive Him through the senses, because he is beyond them. We can feel Him, if we will but withdraw ourselves from the senses. The divine music is incessantly going on within ourselves, but the loud senses down the delicate music, which is unlike and infinitely superior to anything we can perceive or hear with our senses.
>
> — R.K. Prabhu & U.R. Rao (Compiled) : *op. cit.,* pp. 22-23.

The joy of faith living, pulsating, eternal is the joy of the spirit inherent in religion. And Gandhi always makes an introspective analysis of religion with a fusion of spiritualism — a fusion that enables an individual to merge in the millennium. With such a merging with the millennium the contemplation of the Divine Being becomes a reality, an image enkindled with the inner aura of brilliance. It is an exercise of the inner virtues of embracing everyone as an inseparable part of the All Beautiful. The gladness of heart is the gladness of religion in all its practical exposures. As the true spirit of religion inhales a fresh air of faith within each one of us, the existence of perpetual serenity of mind and broadness of vision in uninterrupted cheerfulness becomes an unending partner to humanity in true spiritual endeavour. To stick to such a faith in the spirit of religion is to rediscover the lost island of religion that is never apart from humanity computerized in terms of materialism and numerous abstractions. It is high time to look back at the perennial spirit of religion that makes one humble and dedicated, honest and *sans* selfishness to serve mankind, and thereby himself, better. And if the gift of heaven is the life so precious, it is also the spirit of religion that teaches one how to be happy with the happiness of others. This is to honour both oneself and the religion one endears. Bereft of such a spirit, one's religion is rather ignored or misunderstood. The concept of God, as Gandhi conforms in terms of spiritualism is enriched and poignant in the beyonding of speech and reason, emotion and imagination, intellect and fabrication of facts and ideas. God as the all-pervading spirit transcends all in forms of Love and Truth, Light and Life. Gandhi makes a significant exposition in this connection:

> To me God is Truth and Love, God is ethics and morality, God is fearlessness. God is the source of Light and Life and yet He is above and beyond all these. God is conscience. He is even the atheism of the atheist. * * * He transcends speech and reason. * * * He is a personal God to those who need His personal presence. He is embodied to those who need His touch. He is the purest essence. He simply *is* to those who have faith. He is all things to all men. He is in us and yet above and beyond us. He is long suffering. He is patient but He is also terrible. * * * With Him ignorance is no excuse. And withal He is ever forgiving for He always gives us the chance to repent. He is the greatest democrat the world knows, for He leaves us 'unfettered' to make our own choice between evil and good. He is the greatest tyrant ever known, for He often dashes the cup from our lips and under the cover of free will leaves us a margin so wholly inadequate as to provide only mirth for Himself.
>
> — Pyarelal : *Mahatma Gandhi : The Last Phase*, Navajivan Publishing House, Ahmedabad, Vol. I 1956, pp. 421-422.

The choice between evil and good mixed up in the quagmire of folly and ignorance as religion in the names of fanaticism and separatism presents in profusion, disturbs the inherent conscience of mankind. It simply arrests the beyonding of the self, the Light Eternal, with petty desires and selfish outlook. It discards the 'man' in man and upholds littleness which is a name for conservatism. The spirit of religion, as an unavoidable and inevitable consequence, badly suffers.

Far back in 1934, in a mammoth meeting at Chapra, Bihar on March 27 Gandhi probes deep into the broader spirit of religion that eliminates all narrowness and emphasizes on self-consciousness in the light of the all-pervading spirit of God. Leaving crucial and sharp controversies[1] aside, one cannot but endorse the bond of relationship between the moral and spiritual role of mankind and the indomitable spirit of Nature that serves us the lesson of humility. As Gandhi explains,

> Today a terrible calamity has overwhelmed us all alike — the Hindus, the Musalmans, the Christians and the rest, the so-called high-born and the low-born, without favour of distinction. If even this terrible blow does not enable us to purge ourselves of pride of place and blood, to obliterate all the arbitrary man-made distinctions between man and man, then I would only say that there is none so ill-fated as we. The conviction is growing upon me day after day that human intellect is incapable of fully understanding God's ways. God in His wisdom has circumscribed man's vision, and rightly too, for, otherwise man's conceit would know no bounds. But whilst I believe that God's ways cannot be comprehended fully by man, I have firm faith that not a leaf falls but it subserves His purpose. If only we had enough humility, we would have no hesitation in accepting the recent earthquake as a just retribution for our sins. This is not to say that we can with certainty attribute a particular calamity to a particular human action. Very often we are unconscious of our worst sins. All that I mean to say is that every visitation of nature does and should mean to us nature's call to introspection, repentance and self-purification.
>
> — D.G. Tendulkar : *Mahatma,* Publications Division, M/o I & B, Government of India, Vol. III, p. 255.

The inner spirit of religion and humanism as Gandhi comprehends in his vision of man as the epitome of the All Serene makes a significant contribution to cohesion of spiritualism and religion. In fact, Gandhi as a spiritual apostle makes a radical approach to religion as a great constructive force in elimination of the ills of every aspect of superstition like untouchability. As he categorically observes,

> Is it not shocking to regard the touch of a Musalman or a Christian as unclean, even though he may be as truthful, god-fearing, pure, self-sacrificing and brave as any? God has created different faiths just as He has the votaries thereof. How can I even secretly harbour the thought that my neighbour's faith is inferior to mine? As a true and loyal friend, I can only wish and pray that he may live and grow perfect in his own faith. In God's house there are many mansions and they are all equally holy. All the great religions of the world inculcate the equality and brotherhood of mankind and the virtue of toleration. 'Touch-me-not' ism ** is a morbid growth. It betrays a woodenness of the mind and a blind self-conceit. It is abhorrent alike to the spirit of religion and morality.
>
> —*Ibid.*, p. 257.

Admittedly, Gandhi goes deep into the inner concept of religion as a basic component of human civilization. He adores religion not because it has a superior force within but primarily because it is the most dependable symbol of human consciousness for beyonding of being. As a true exponent of religion, he feels oneness with God not by alienation from but by closeness to humanity under all trying circumstances — varied, complex and, therefore, thrilling and dramatic. A betrayal to the essential unity of all religions as Gandhi strongly believes, is a betrayal to spiritualism. In fact, an ennobling spirit of religion has adorned his vision of non-violence which is actually the vision of the true spirit of the oneness of humanity. That is why he cannot accept the dissection of the eternal bonds of unit backed by age-old culture. Tradition and heritage of humanism. As he strongly reacts against vivisection in terms of religion:

> As a man of non-violence, I cannot forcibly resist the proposed partition, if the Muslims of India really insist upon it. But, I never can be a willing party to the vivisection. I would employ every non-violent means to prevent it. For it means the undoing of centuries of work done by numberless Hindus and Muslims to live

> together as one nation. Partition means a patent untruth. My whole soul revels against the idea that Hinduism and Islam represent to antagonistic cultures and doctrines. To assent to such a doctrine is for me denial of God. For I believe with my whole soul that the God of the Koran is also the God of the Gita, and that we are all, no matter by what name designated, children of the same God. I must rebel against the idea that millions of Indians who were Hindus that other day changed their nationality on adopting Islam as their religion.
>
> But that is my belief. I cannot thrust it down the throats of the Muslims who think that they are a different nation. I refuse, however, to believe that the eight crores of Muslims will say that they have nothing in common with their Hindu and other brethren. Their mind can only be known by a referendum made to them only on that clear issue.
>
> — D.G. Tendulkar : *Mahatma, op. cit.,* p. 271.

The basic factors of Gandhian religion are primarily geared towards understanding and actualising the spiritual values of mankind. Truth as a religious force acts as a compass in adapting, gradually but surely, towards fullness of humanity. Moreover, as a moral force, religion serves the twin purpose of self-purification, and appreciation to and endearment of all beliefs. Whether we term such concept of Gandhian religion as basic or otherwise, the fact remains clear that Gandhi crystallizes the whole arena of religion with a view to making a unison between religion and spiritualism from multi-dimensional facets of Truth, non-violence, *Swaraj* or *nai talim* as the case might be.

> Gandhi's religion is basic in three aspects, First, in the breadth and depth of its definition of ultimate Reality as Truth, Second, in its insistence that religion is all pervasive and not a compartmental concern. And third, in its unreserved acceptance of validity of all religious.
>
> — S.K. George : 'Basic Religion : A study in Gandhi's Religion'; Kshitis Roy (Ed) : *The Visva-Bharati Quarterly,* Gandhi Memorial Peace Number, Santiniketan, 1949, p. 96.

To feel the existence of God as the ocean of Love is the first lesson of spiritualism as Gandhi emphasizes as an outcome of religion. For him everyone is an *upasak* — a worshipper — trying continually to crystallize himself as the son of *amrita.* to such a spiritual seeker as Gandhi portrays, love heals the wounds of the self as well as those of humanity. As he strongly asserts,

> Religion does not teach not to bear ill-will towards one another. It is easy enough to be friendly to one's friends. But to befriend the one who regards himself as your enemy, is the quintessence of true religion.
>
> — M.K. Gandhi : *Harijan,* May 11, 1947.

Delving deep into the essence of spiritualism in religion, Gandhi finds a universal truth of the march of mankind as an earnest seeker of humanism. The faith that each individual nursles within his own religious domain is never antagonistic to other faiths derived or endeared in other religions. For, all religions enable us to foster within ourselves the most prized spiritual enlightenment. As such, the vision of a truly religious thinker cannot but welcome the light of inner awareness. Gandhi's own experience of spiritual awakening through diverse religious pursuit deserves rethinking in right earnest:

> * * * I have come to the conclusion that (1) all religions are true; (2) all religions have some error in them; (3) all religions are almost as dear to me as my own Hinduism, inasmuch as all human beings should be as dear to one as one's own close relatives. My own veneration for other faiths is the same as that for my own faith; therefore, no thought of conversion in possible. The aim of the fellowship should be to help a Hindu to become a better Hindu, a Musalman to become a better Musalman, and a Christian a better Christian. The attitude of patronizing toleration is false to the spirit of International Fellowship. If I have a suspicion in my mind that my religion is more or less true, and that others' are more or less false, instead of being more or less true, then, though I may have some sort of fellowship with them, it is of an entirely different kind from the one we need in the International Fellowships. Our prayer for other must be NOT 'God, give him the light that Thou hast given me, BUT, 'Give him all the light and truth he needs for his highest development'. Pray merely that your friends may become better men, whatever their form of

religion.

Nevertheless, your experience may become a part of their experience, without your knowing it.

— M.K. Gandhi : *Report of the Annual Meeting of the Federation of International Fellowships,* Satyagraha Ashram, Sabarmati, January 13-15. 1928, Federation of International Fellowship, Sabarmati, 1928, p. 17.

When Gandhi wants to inculcate the inner essence of religion he takes recourse to the enrichment of aesthetic sensibilities so that spiritualism becomes a dynamic part of religious efflorescence. Truth, then, shines out as one of the fundamental outcomes of religion. The inherent beauty of every religion exercised in all earnestness by an individual brings forth a certain depth of vision born in the womb of tolerance that very significantly takes its role in the onward progress of mankind. The fusion between truth and God, as Gandhi time and again emphasizes, is the fusion that bears the true stamp of cohesion between spiritualism and religion. A modern world, worriedly awaiting the blend of mutual faiths amid different religions cannot but look back in optimism by means of the Gandhian guidelines of tolerance. As he poignantly observes,

Tolerance may imply a gratuitous assumption of the inferiority of the other faith to one's own, whereas *ahimsa* teaches us to entertain the same respect for the religious faiths as others as we accord to our own, thus admitting the imperfection of the latter. This admission will be readily made by a seeker of Truth who follows the law of Love. If we had attained the full vision of Truth, we would no longer be mere seekers, but have become one with God, for Truth is God. But being only seekers, we prosecute our quest, and are conscious of our imperfection. And if we are imperfect ourselves, religion as conceived by us must also be imperfect. We have not realized religion in its imperfection, even as we have not realized God. Religion of our conception, being thus imperfect, is always subject to a process of evolution and reinterpretation. Progress towards Truth, towards God, is possible only because of such evolution. And if all faiths outlined by men are imperfect, the question of comparative merit does not arise. All faiths constitute a revelation of Truth, but all are imperfect,

> and liable to error. Reverence for others' faiths need not blind us to their faults. We must be keenly alive to the defects of our own faith also, yet not leave it on that account, but try to overcome those defects. Looking at all religions with an equal eye, we would not only not hesitate, but would think it our duty, to blend into our faith every acceptable feature of other faiths.
>
> — M.K. Gandhi : *From Yeravda Mandir, op. cit.*, p. 55.

A living sense of evolution of consciousness as one of the most desirable components of spiritualism cannot, as Gandhi deeply feels, but be incorporated in religion so that religion never comes down to the level of orthodoxy or fanaticism, Nor should religion be ever diverted towards negotiating a particular sect, caste, creed or community at the cost of others. Truth, unending Truth, must act as a torch-bearer to every religion that will always speak in the language of Love. Every religion then will be instrumental to awakening of good sense and sensibilities. Hatred and ill-feeling, then, will, certainly be over-powered by the religion of co-operation and sympathy. With such an evolution of consciousness for the welfare of all, — *Sarve sukhino bhavantu, sarve santu niramayah,* (let everyone be happy, let everyone be *sans* sufferings) — the spirit of religion embraces altruism. Gandhi directs his spiritualistic vision of religion with such a positive approach to the welfare of one and all and the *Sarvodaya,* the awakening of all, as he launches as a movement is a promise of perfection in dedication to God'. Professor V.K.R.V. Rao makes a significant observation on how Gandhi channelizes *Sarvodaya* for such a spiritual awakening through a classless society:

> *Sarvodaya,* the welfare of all, is a classless society based on the destruction of classes but not on the destruction of the individuals who constitute the classes, a system of production that does not fail to make use of science and technology for creating an economy of abundance but does not in the process either kill individual initiative or freedom from development or create a psychology of ceaseless striving for more and more material gods, a system of distribution that will ensure a reasonable minimum income for all, and while not aiming at a universal equality of an arithmetical kind, will nevertheless ensure that all private property or talent beyond the minimum will be used as a trust for

> the public good and not for individual aggrandisement, a social order where all will work but there is not inequality, either in status or in opportunity for any individual, and a political system where change is the result of persuasion, differences are resolved by discussion, and conflict by love and recognition of mutuality of interest and a life spent in dedication to God and cultivation of the spirit.
>
> — V.K.R.V. Rao : *The Gandhian Alternative to Western Socialism,* Bharatiya Vidya Bhavan, Bombay, 1981, p. 47.

The inherent force of religion in the form of spiritual efflorescence serves as a guideline to the Gandhian concept of *Sarvodaya.* That is why Gandhi's religion is the religion of dedication of oneself towards the welfare of others. In fact, his idea of *Sarvodaya* incorporates this spirit of dedication which he describes as *pararthabhavana* endearing the All serene in humility. As Gandhi splendidly elucidates,

> Our existence as embodied beings is purely momentary; what are a hundred years in eternity? But if we shatter the chains of egotism, and melt into the ocean of humanity, we share its dignity. To feel that we are something is to set up a barrier between God and ourselves; to cease feeling that we are something is to become one with God. A drop in the ocean partakes of the greatness of its parent, although it is unconscious of it. But it is dried up as soon as it enters upon an existence independent of the ocean. * * *
>
> God is continuously in action without resting for a single moment. If we would serve Him or become one with Him, our activity must be as unwearied as His. There may be momentary rest in store for the drop which is separated from the ocean, but not for the drop in the ocean, which knows no rest. The same is the case with ourselves. As soon as we become one with the ocean in the shape of God, there is no more rest for us, nor indeed do we need rest any longer. Our very sleep is action. For we sleep with the thought of God in our hearts. This restlessness constitutes true rest. This never ceasing agitation holds the key to peace ineffable. This supreme state of total surrender is difficult to describe, but not beyond the bounds of human experience. It has been attained by many dedicated souls, and may be attained by our-

selves as well.

— M.K. Gandhi : *From Yeravda Mandir, op. cit.*, p. 126.

With such an enlightened view of religion in the pattern of *Sarvodaya* that directs an individual to think and act for the welfare of others, Gandhi widens the spiritual outlook of religion by diffusion of differences in upholding an optimistic view. To him, religion in the true sense of the term, is always a light that enkindles the inner self and brings forth endless joy. As he categorically remarks,

> I have not been able to see any difference between the Sermon on the Mount and the *Bhagvadgita*. What the Sermon describes in a graphic manner, the *Bhagvadgita* reduces to a scientific formula. It may not be a scientific book in the accepted sense of the term, but it has argued out of the law of love — the law of abandon as I would call it — in a scientific manner. The Sermon on the Mount gives the same law in wonderful language. The New Testament gave me comfort and boundless joy, as it came after the repulsion that parts of the Old had given me. Today supposing I was deprived of the Gita and forget all its contents but had a copy of the Sermon, I should derive the same joy from it as I do from the *Gita*.
>
> * * * I love to see the bright side of things and not the seamy side, and so I can derive comfort and inspiration from any great book of any great religion. I may not be able to reproduce a single verse from the Gita or the New Testament, a Hindu child or Christian child may be able to repeat the verses better, but those clever children cannot deprive me of the assimilation that is in me today of the spirit of the two books.

— M.K. Gandhi : *Young India*, December 22, 1927.

Firmly rooted in the teachings of the *Gita*, the religion that Gandhi highlights is the religion of emancipation from all selfish attitudes. It is the religion that accelerates the eternal march of man towards perfection — the ascent of man as spiritualism stands for. The lesson that one learns from true religion is how to win over oneself or one's ego that awaits emancipation in altruism. Gandhi's own explanation on this point is as follows:

> There is no man who is governed exclusively by one of the three *gunas —sattva, raja* and *tamas*. We have each of us to rise to a state in which we are governed predominantly by the *sattva* principle, until at last we rise beyond the three and are 'Perfect Man'. I can think of an illustration from the physical world. Take water, which in its solid state remains on the earth; it cannot ascend until it is rarefied into steam. But once it is rarefied into steam it rises up in the sky where at last it is transformed into clouds which drop down in the form of rain and fructify and bless the earth. We are all like water, we have to strive so to rarefy ourselves that all the ego in us perishes and we merge in the Infinite to the eternal good of all.
>
> —*Ibid.*, January 12, 1928.

The elimination of the ego, as Gandhi strongly advocates is the way to perfection — the way every human being should all the time tread on for realization of Truth, which is God. The spiritual vision of God as a living force that draws upon man is the only prized religion that man must aim at to become one in unison with the All Beautiful. Gandhi, therefore, urges for the discovery of that Living Force in us:

> God is not a person. * * * God is the force. He is the essence of life. He is pure and undefiled consciousness. He is eternal and yet, strangely enough, all are not able to derive either benefit from or shelter in the all-pervading living presence.
>
> Electricity is a powerful force. Not all can benefit from it. It can only be produced by following certain laws. It is a lifeless force. Man can utilize it if he labours hard enough to acquire the knowledge of its laws.
>
> The living force which we call God can similarly be found if we know and follow His law leading to the discovery of Him in us.
>
> — Pyarelal : *Mahatma Gandhi, op. cit.,* Vol. I, 1956, p. 599.

How, then, can one be attuned to the Living Force within oneself? As an humble seeker of Truth, Gandhi emphasizes on prayer that gradually turns one to be worthy of union with the Living Force. His exposition in this connection is significant :

> I started with disbelief in God and prayer, and until at a later stage in life I did not feel anything like a void in life. But at that

stage, I felt that as food is indispensable for the body, so was prayer indispensable for the soul. For starvation is often necessary to keep the body in health, but there is no such thing as prayer starvation. You cannot probably have a surfeit of prayer. Three of the greatest teachers of the world — Buddha, Jesus and Muhammad — have left unimpeachable testimony, that they found illumination through prayer and could not possibly live without it. Millions of Hindus, Musalmans and Christians find their only solace in life in prayer. Either you call them liars or self-deluded people. I will say that this 'lying' has a charm for me a truth-seeker, if it is 'lying' that has given me that mainstay or staff of life without which I could not live for a moment. In spite of despair staring me in the face on the political horizon, I have never lost my peace. In fact I have found people who envy my peace. That peace comes from prayer. I am not a man of learning, but I humbly claim to be a man of prayer. I am indifferent as to the form. Everyone is a law unto himself in that respect. But there are some well-marked roads, and it is safe to walk along the beaten tracks, trodden by the ancient teachers. I have given my personal testimony. Let everyone try and find that as a result of daily prayer he adds something new to his life.

— D.G. Tendulkar : *Mahatma, op. cit.,* Vol. III, 1952, pp. 139-140.

Are we prepared to respond to the above?

NOTE

1. In this connection, Rabindranath Tagore's sharp rejoinder to Gandhi's utterances on the earthquake is very significant:

"It has caused me a painful surprise to find Mahatma Gandhi accusing those who blindly follow their own social custom of un-touchability, of having brought down God's vengeance upon certain parts of Bihar, evidently, specially selected for His desolating displeasure. It is all the more unfortunate, because this kind of unscientific view of phenomena is too readily accepted by a large section of our countrymen. I keenly feel the indignity of it, when I am compelled to utter a truism in asserting that the physical catastrophies have their inevitable and exclusive origin in certain combination of the physical facts. Unless we believe in the inexorableness of the universal law in the working of which God Himself never interferes, we find it impossible to justify His ways on an occasion like the one which has sorely stricken us in an overwhelming manner and scale.

If we associate ethical principles with the cosmic phenomena, we shall have to admit that human nature is morally much superior to Providence that preaches its lessons in good behaviour in orgies of the worst behaviour possible. For, we can never imagine any civilized ruler of men making indiscriminate examples of casual victims including children and the members of the untouchable community, in order to impress other dwelling at a safe distance, who possibly deserve more severe condemnation. Though we cannot point out any period of human history that is free from inequities of the darkest kind, we still find citadels of malevolence yet remain unshaken, that the factories that cruelly thrive upon abject poverty and ignorance of the famished cultivators, or prison-houses in all parts of the world where a penal system is pursued, which, most often, is a special form of special criminality, still stand firm. It only shows that the law of gravitation does not in the least respond to the stupendous load of callousness that accumulates till the moral foundation of our society begins to show dangerous cracks and civilizations are undermined. What is truly tragic about it is the fact that the kind of argument the Mahatmaji used by exploiting an event of cosmic disturbance far better suits the psychology of his opponents than his own, and it would not have surprised me, if they had taken this opportunity of holding him and his followers responsible for the visitation of divine anger. As for us, we feel perfectly secure in the faith that our sins and errors, however enormous, have not enough force to drag down the structure of creation to ruins. We can depend upon it, sinners and saints, bigots and breakers of convention. And we, who are immensely grateful to Mahatmaji for inducing by his wonder-working inspiration, freedom from fear and feebleness in the minds of his countrymen, feel profoundly hurt, when any words from his mouth may emphasize the elements of unreason in those very minds, unreason, which is a fundamental source of all the blind powers that drive us against freedom and self-respect".

— Quoted from D.G. Tendulkar : *Mahatma,* Publications Division, Ministry of Information and Broadcasting, Government of India, Vol. III, pp. 247-248.

6

GANDHIAN SPIRITUALISM: The Mystic Dimensions

Spiritualism, the lost language of modernity, is the only way to negotiate the inherent ukase in man. The Lotus-land of purity is the heart-land of human consciousness as true spiritualism awaits a rebirth or a reincarnation in the journey of beyonding of consciousness. The delight of Truth as a mystic force in beauty is actually the delight one receives out of the infinite wonder of the universe as an intrinsic appreciating urge.

Like a mystic visionary, Gandhi allows spiritualism to be serenely married to mysticism. He makes a deeper probe into the world of delight amid beauty in appreciation to Nature. The poignance thus ingrained in human consciousness can present us with such a world of beauty as Gandhi visualizes in art:

> All true art must help the soul to realize its inner self. In my own case, I find that I can do entirely without the external forms in my soul's realization. Therefore, I can claim, that there is truly sufficient art in my life, though you might not see what you call works of art about me. My room may have blank walls; and I may even dispense with the roof, so that I may gaze out upon the starry heavens overhead that stretch in an unending expanse of beauty. What conscious art of man can give me the panoramic scene that opens out before me, when I look up to the sky above with all its shining stars? This, however, does not mean that I refuse to accept the value of productions of art, generally accepted as such, but only that I personally feel the eternal symbols of beauty in nature. These productions of man's art have their value only in so far as they help the soul onward towards self-realization.

–D.G. Tendulkar: *Mahatma, op. cit.*, Vol. II, p. 159.

Furthermore, Gandhi adds the mystic dimension to spiritualism in elucidating art as follows:

> Indeed, these beauties are truthful, inasmuch as they make me think of the Creator at the back of them. How also could these be beautiful but for the truth that is the centre of creation? when I admire the wonder of a sunset or the beauty of the moon, my soul expands in worship of the Creator. I try to see Him and His mercies in all these creations. But even the sunsets and sunrises would be mere hindrances, if they did not help me to think of Him. Any-thing which is a hindrance to the flight of the soul, is a delusion and a snare; even, like the body, which often does hinder you in the path of salvation.
>
> –*Ibid.*, p. 160.

'The flight of the soul', the salvation of the man *par excellence* through purity and perfection is the core of Gandhian spiritualism that incorporates the mystic consciousness of man. For this, a look within and a look for beyonding of that introspective endeavour are both mandatory. Truth, as a spiritual force, actually shows this efflorescence of mystic awareness. When Gandhi expands the spiritual vision of God as Truth, he actually broadens it by incorporating the mystic dimension of Truth. Like a mystico-spiritualist, Gandhi himself admits that he has 'grown from Truth to Truth'. The sense of spiritual joy that he derives out of Truth is indeed an inward vision that only a true mystic like him can encounter. Admittedly, he comes nearer to the mystic vision of Sri Aurobindo who emphasizes on the power of the spirit as the beckoner of inward Light to traverse on the unending Lotus-land of Joy.[1] Perhaps Gandhi is more aware of the inner being and its transcendence towards nobler and deeper truth than bare practicalities with which Truth is more often than not, confounded. Truth as the exposer of inner worth is actually the truth of the 'inner voice of God' that Gandhi himself experiences all the time as an humble servant of mankind. The strategy he adopts to arrive at such a mystico-spiritual state of mind is self-purification which as he deeply feels, opens the inward vision and enables him to clearly listen to the still small voice within. As he observes,

> Having made a ceaseless effort to attain self-purification, I have developed some little capacity to hear correctly and clearly the

still small voice within.

– Pyarelal: *The Epic Past*, Mohanlal Maganlal Bhatt, Ahmedabad, p. 34.

Gandhi is well aware of the fact that the essence of spiritualism lies in diverse mystic dimensions. The lost soul of humanity is never the soul lost but it is to be regained in the consciousness of the living soul – the spiritual soul or the soul that is enshrined in the temple of humanism. A worthy return to the roots of human consciousness essentially demands a mystic approach to life so that the higher feelings and the nobler sentiments of life are translated into the true efflorescence of humanism. This, then, is Gandhian spiritualism that highlights mysticism from three-fold avenues of awareness. First, one must strive for becoming a true inheritor of the Kingdom of Being, the Kingdom that breaks all barriers of the essence of humanity. Secondly, the veils of ignorance are to be cast aside from the mind that should always keep all the windows of good sense and sensibilities wide open. Thirdly, the mind of an individual must be allowed to enjoy and to be enjoyed with, the ecstatic joy of emancipation from all shortcomings of life. The promise of individual efflorescence is the goal of mysticism which Gandhi serenely incorporates in his concept of spiritualism. Spratt makes a very significant observation on Gandhi as a mystico-spiritual visionary:

> The voice is always preceded by an acute and painful internal struggle and its occurrence, which is followed by internal peace, always represents a decision which it would be painful to reach and difficult to justify by ordinary thought. It is religiously or spiritually true. This effect of this voice is to render its injunction sacred, to safeguard it against criticism, by himself or others, and against laziness or any fleshly impediment. The voice thus partakes of the nature of conscience, but it cannot be identified with conscience. * * * * The conscience is satisfied by an appeal to ordinary principles or modes of feeling. This voice seems to speak for an extra or pseudo-conscience, and suggest an extravagant sort of act, usually a fast, which is commonly subject to suspicion as to its motives, and is such that Mr. Gandhi's normal puritanical conscience might very well not approve of it.

–P. Spratt: *Gandhism: An Analysis*, Huxley Press, Madras. p. 363.

The mystic 'inner voice' that Gandhi always attends to, is the inner strength that teaches him the true lesson of spiritualism. The religion that he advocates, teaches him that lesson which allows him to evolve from time to time to be pure in thought and action, promise and performance. In fact, his spiritual vision of non-violence as a great mystic force is a ceaseless endeavour on his part to cultivate the inner essence of consciousness not as an ascetic but as an ordinary man striving for perfection. His own verdict on this point serves a better exposure:

> It is wrong to call me an ascetic. The ideals that regulate my life are presented for acceptance by mankind in general. I have arrived at them by gradual evolution. Every step was thought out, well-considered, and taken with the greatest deliberation. Both my continence and non-violence were derived from personal experience and became necessary in response to the calls of public duty. The isolated life I had to lead in South Africa whether as a householder, legal practitioner, social reformer or politician, required for the due fulfilment of these duties, the strictest regulation of sexual life and a rigid practice of non-violence and truth in human relations, whether with my own countrymen or with the Europeans. I claim to be no more than an average man with less than average ability. Nor can I claim any special merit for such non-violence or continence as I have been able to reach with laborious research. I have not the shadow of a doubt that any man or woman can achieve what I have, if he or she would make the same effort and cultivate the same hope and faith.
>
> – M.K. Gandhi: *Harijan*, October 3, 1936.

The cultivation of hope and faith by means of non-violence as a soul-force is, indeed, the cultivation of consciousness that fillips one's spiritual growth. It is as Gandhi believes, to be always bourne in mind that such a sincere cultivation will bring about a desirable change of mass awareness to self-purification by means of gradual evolution within every being. As an optimist, he, therefore, calls for the inner appreciation to infinite human possibilities which will certainly steer one towards introspection as a mystic visionary:

> My optimism rests on on my belief in the infinite possibilities of

> the individual to develop non-violence. The more you develop it in our own being, the more infectious it becomes till it overwhelms your surroundings and by and by might oversweep the world.
>
> – R.K. Prabhu & U.R. Rao (Complied): *op. cit.*, p. 46.

The explore the infinite possibilities of an individual amidst self-preparation and self-suffering is the dynamic aspect that Gandhi evolves through non-violence and this evolution of consciousness makes an individual bold enough to fight against all evils and come out victorious with the indomitable role of the soul-force within himself. This is what a truly spiritual person always strives for emancipation of goodness in the world. He remains conscious of all sufferings and trying circumstances. For, the quest that he makes within is the quest for the eternal blessings of the All Beautiful. It is a quest for the merging of man with the Supreme Being, when self-realization finds its ultimate aroma of fulfilment. This mystic vision of non-violence as a dynamic force finds appropriate elucidation in Gandhi's own words as follows:

> Non-violence in its dynamic condition means conscious suffering. It does not mean meek submission to the will of the evil-doer, but it means the putting of one's whole soul against the will of the tyrant. Working under this law of our being, it is possible for a single individual to defy the whole might of an unjust empire to save his honour, his religion, his soul, and lay the foundation for that empire's fall or its regeneration.
>
> – M.K. Gandhi: *Young India*, August 11, 1920.

That *ahimsa* or non-violence is not a weapon of the weak but of the strong incorporates the spiritual vision of harmonization of all where the mystic sensibilities of elimination of all narrowness of outlook and expansion of the mind for the beyonding of consciousness play a very significant role to shatter all encumbrances like fear, enmity and so on. Love bestowed and love received arrive at a platform of unison as a positive mystico-spiritual force in the active pursuit of *ahimsa*. This love armoured with a certain sense of promise of security within, enjoys a warm embrace, a bliss endless and unassuming. Gandhi makes a fine analysis:

> If I am a follower of *ahimsa*, I *must love* my enemy. I must apply the same rules to the wrong-doer who is my enemy or a stranger to me, as I would to my wrong-doing father or son. This active *ahimsa* necessarily includes truth and fearlessness. As man cannot deceive the loved one, he does not fear or frighten him or her. Gift of life is the greatest of all gifts; a man who gives it in reality, disarms all hostility. He has paved the way for an honourable understanding. And none who is himself subject to fear can bestow that gift. He must therefore be himself fearless. A man cannot practise *ahimsa* and be a coward at the same time. The practice of *ahimsa* calls forth the greatest courage.
>
> – M.K. Gandhi: *Speeches and Writings of Mahatma Gandhi*, G.A. Natesan & Co., Madras, p. 346.

The crusade against violence that Gandhi makes is a spiritual crusade backed by the mystic aspect of eluding the propagator of violence with the awareness of goodness within himself. Gandhi calls 'the resistance of the soul' the best weapon to resist evil, because the inward awakening of the soul of the evil-doer will certainly bring forth the desirable sense of humility – an essence of mystic aura of consciousness. The spirit eternal for goodness of all comes out in all illuminating grandeur, for the liberation of the soul of an individual no longer remains a myth. Indeed, non-violence as Gandhi in his mystic vision foresees, is a real involvement – a fight genuine and stirring revolution – with mental and moral propensities. As he categorically observes,

> Non-violence is 'not a resignation from all real fighting against wickedness'. On the contrary, the non-violence of my conception is a more active and real fight against wickedness than retaliation whose very nature is to increase wickedness. I contemplate a mental and therefore a moral opposition to immoralities. I seek entirely to blunt the edge of the tyrant's sword, not by putting up against it a sharper-edged weapon, but by disappointing his expectation that I would be offering physical resistance. The resistance of the soul that I should offer would elude him. It would at first dazzle him, which recognition would not humiliate him but

would uplift him. It may be urged that this is an ideal state. And so it is.

– M.K. Gandhi: *Young India*, October 8, 1925.

As a mystic visionary, Gandhi applies this spiritual force in the form of *Satyagraha* because he firmly believes that the mystic light of consciousness cannot but eliminate the darkness of all evil forces. It is better than any other force because the inherent sense of goodness is never lost nor is it ever allowed to be dwarfed by violence as such. The follower of *satyagraha* is spiritually armoured with the weapon of self-determination and belief in the infinite strength of man, which knows no defeat. Gandhi's own exposition in this connection may be referred:

> Carried out to its utmost limit, this force is independent of pecuniary or other material assistance, certainly, even in its elementary form, of physical force or violence. Indeed, violence is the negation of this great spiritual force which can only be cultivated or wielded by those who will entirely eschew violence. It is a force that may be used by individuals as well as by communities. It may be used as well in political as in domestic affairs. Its universal applicability is a demonstration of its permanence and invincibility. It can be used alike by men, women and children. It is totally untrue to say that it is a force to be used only by the weak so long as they are not capable of meeting violence by violence. This superstition arises from the incompleteness of the English expression. It is impossible for those who consider themselves to be weak to apply this force. Only those who realize that there is something in man which is superior to the brute nature in him, and that the latter always yields to it, can effectively be passive resisters. This force is to violence and, therefore to all tyranny all injustice, what light is to darkness.
>
> – M.K. Gandhi: *Harijan*, July 21, 1940.

The infinite strength of man to overcome his limitations and endear the Rose of God as Sri Aurobindo introspects as a spiritual visionary[2] also finds a very poignant appeal in Gandhi's spiritualism. He also makes a unison between man and the All Beautiful bearing in mind the importance of extinction of personality. Like a serene mystic he observes,

> Our existence as embodied beings is purity momentary; what are a hundred years in eternity? But if we shatter the chains of egotism, and melt into the ocean of humanity, we share its dignity. To feel that we are something is to set up a barrier between God and ourselves; to cease feeling that we are something is to become one with God.
>
> – M.K. Gandhi: *From Yeravda Mandir*, Navajivan Press, Ahmedabad, 1935, p. 68.

Looking upon austerity as an intensive spiritual exercise, Gandhi directs towards inwardness of vision by means of the mystic concept of God as Truth and Love. This is, indeed, a synchronized pattern of consciousness when the spirit of God within man finds a new language of expression, a new light of awareness. With this new spiritual vision man makes an endless adventure into the heartland of yearning for the all-abiding grace of the Rose of God. A revelation of affluence amidst apparent austerity is an unending mystic grandeur. Gandhi as a mystic, wants to uphold that grandeur:

> Not for the enjoyment of this life, but for the enjoyment of personal service to your fellow being, service to which you dedicate yourselves, body, soul and mind. * * * * Even the body is not yours. It has been given to you as a temporary possession and it can also be taken from you by Him who has given it to you.
>
> Therefore, having that absolute conviction in me, such must be my constant desire that this body also may be surrendered at the will of God, and while it is at my disposal must be used not for pleasure, but merely for service and service, the whole of your working hours. And if this is true with reference to the body, how much more with reference to clothing and other things that we use?
>
> And those who have followed out this vow of voluntary poverty to the fullest extent possible – to reach absolute perfection is an impossibility, but the fullest possible extent of a human being – those who have reached the ideal of that state, they testify that when you dispossess yourself of everything you have, you really

possess all the treasures of the word.

– D.G. Tendulkar: *Mahatma, op. cit.,* Vol. III, pp. 124-125.

Why does Gandhi resort to passive resistance? One of the main reasons for adhering to non-violence is to enkindle conscience as a soul-force – an inward efflorescence of spiritualism by means of mystic vision. Explaining his method of passive resistance, he spells out how it acts as an inward component of soul-force in embracing self-suffering for an awakening of all-round good sense and sensibilities:

> Passive resistance is a method of securing rights by personal suffering; it is the reverse of resistance by arms. When I refuse to do a thing that is repugnant to my conscience, I use soul-force. * * * * If I do not obey the law and accept the penalty for its breach, I use soul-force. It involves sacrifice of self.
>
> Everybody admits that sacrifice of self is infinitely superior to sacrifice of others. Moreover, if this kind of force is used in a cause that is unjust, only the person using it suffers. He does not make others suffer for his mistakes. Men have before now done many things which were subsequently found to have been wrong. No men can claim that he is absolutely in the right or that a particular thing is wrong because he thinks so, but it is wrong for him so long as that is his deliberate judgement. It is therefore meet that he should not do that which he knows to be wrong, and suffer the consequence whatever it may be. This is the key to the use of soul-force.

– M.K. Gandhi: *Hind Swaraj or Indian Home Rule*, Navajivan Publishing House, Ahmedabad, 1944, p. 45.

The spiritual weapon of self-suffering for self-purification is as Gandhi believes, the outcome of a mystic vision of revolution for rapid evolution of human consciousness. As a consequence, goodness arrived at through non-violence is more desirable for spiritual efflorescence than even victory by coercion and force. The world bruised and battered, cannot but encourage such goodness to be nursed by every individual as an embodiment of Spirit Eternal. As Gandhi significantly observes:

> Good brought through force destroyed individuality. Only when the change was effected through the persuasive power of non-violent non-cooperation, i.e., love, could the foundation of individuality be preserved, and real, abiding progress be assured for the world.
>
> – M.K. Gandhi: *Harijan*, March 9, 1947.

Elsewhere,

> I do not deny the revolutionary's heroism and sacrifice. But heroism and sacrifice in a bad cause are so much waste of splendid energy and hurt the good cause by drawing away attention from it by the glamour of the misused heroism and sacrifice in a bad cause.
>
> I am not ashamed to stand erect before the heroic and self-sacrificing revolutionary because I am able to pit an equal measure of non-violent men's heroism and sacrifice untarnished by the blood of the innocent. Self-sacrifice of one innocent man is a million times more potent than the sacrifice of million men who die in the act of killing others. The willing sacrifice of the innocent is the most powerful retort to insolent tyranny that has yet been conceived by God or man.
>
> – M.K. Gandhi: *Young India*, February 12, 1925.

A superior and intense process, working subtly and invisibly as a mystico-spiritual force, non-violence as Gandhi launches, is actually a weapon not to hurt anybody but to bring about a change of consciousness that enables everyone to exceed himself through self-surrender and self-purification. It is a weapon to be truly spiritual to open the mind to great possibilities by filling it with sublime ideas. It is also a weapon that warns an individual to save his soul by igniting the spirit within. Gandhi accentuates the force of the soul by means of non-violence fundamentally from his mystic vision of God as enshrined in man in the manifold components of love, service and sacrifice. His life-long experience with Truth shows the inward mystic light that conforms exquisitely with the fact that God never needs anything except the 'man' in man – the man that represents truth and God at the same time. Such a *Satyanarayana* — a mystic concept of man representing God – highlights the Gandhian principle of spiritualism in the most practical fashion. As a matter of fact, Gandhi unfolds a newer avenue of spiritualism by allowing himself to work in the meleé of the mob as a practical mystic to visualize everyone as an inseparable and indivisible part of God.

The spiritual and vital growth that nursles the mystic vision of Gandhi who considers non-violence as a ceaseless growth within echoes the mystic vision of Shri Aurobindo:

> However the man of spiritual realisation lives and acts and behaves, in all ways of his being and acting . * * * * he lives in the Divine. In our present life of Nature, in our externalized surface existence, it is the world that seems to create us; but in the turn to the spiritual life it is we who must create ourselves and our world. In this new formula of creation, the inner life becomes of the first importance and the rest can be only its expression and outcome. It is this, indeed, that is indicated by our own strivings towards perfection, the perfection of our own soul, and mind and life and the perfection of the life of the race. For we are given a world which is obscure, ignorant, material, imperfect, and our external conscious being is itself created by its energies, the pressure, the moulding operations of the vast mute obscurity, by physical birth, by environment, by a training through the impacts and shocks of life; and yet are vaguely aware of something that is there in us or seeking to be, something other than what has been thus made, a spirit self-existent, self-determining, pushing the nature towards the image of its own occult perfection or idea of perfection. There is something that grows in answer to this demand, that strives to become the image of a divine somewhat, and is impelled also to labour at the world outside that has been given to it and remake that too in a greater image, in the image of its own spiritual and mental and vital growth, to make our world into something created according to our own mind and self-conceiving spirit, something new, harmonious, perfect.
>
> – Sri Aurobindo: *The Life Divine*, Sri Aurobindo Ashram, Pondicherry.

The inherent spirit of life revealed in exercise of Truth and non-violence as Gandhi wants to introduce in day to day activities elevates an individual from dwarfness of mind and pulsates with the harmonizing spirit of humane sensibilities. A sombre promise of the Endless in mystic poignance brings one nearer to the Innermost One within oneself. In fact, Gandhi as a spiritual visionary of God in the image of Truth or Non-violence as a mystic force comes closer to Rabindranath Tagore who unfolds the mystic vision of the All Beautiful in the splendid aroma of poignance as follows:

> He it is, the innermost one, who awakens my being with his deep hidden touches.
>
> He it is who puts his enchantment upon these eyes and joyfully plays on the chords of my heart in varied cadence of pleasure and pain.
>
> He it is who weaves the web of this *maya* in evanescent hues of gold and silver, blue and green, and lets peep out through the folds his feet, at whose touch I forget myself.
>
> Days come and ages pass, and it is ever he who moves my heart in many a name, in many a guise, in many a rapture of joy and of sorrow.
>
> – Rabindranath Tagore: *Song Offerings (Gitanjali)*, Macmillan India Limited, Macmillan Pocket Tagore Edition, 1983 No. LXXII, pp. 48-49.

A mystic visionary *par excellence*, Gandhi also wants humanity to be purified in best ideas, best thoughts and best sensibilities. Whatever appears to be impure and imperfect either in an individual or in life and society necessitates an inward change which can alone take place in the unending practice of perfection. As a spiritual crusader, Gandhi crushes aside the curse of age-old superstitions as exposed either in sham religious and social stratas of life or in observance of life in an undesirable and immoral manner *sans* aesthetic and mystical poignance of vision. With soul-force as the great mystic vision of a spiritual aspirant, he has proved how a great social ill like untouchability can be eliminated. And, even if, for such a mystic and spiritual fulfilment, one cannot but embrace martyrdom, he should prefer to do so because a martyr for such a great cause remains an eternal example of mystic emancipation for posterity. In this connection, one might recall Gandhi's glowing tribute to Swami Shraddhanandaji who died as a valiant crusader against untouchability by preaching the lesson of love for all mankind:

> A great hero and patriot, Swami Shraddhanandaji, died for the sake of the untouchables. He loved them as his own children, and if it was in his power, he would have banished untouchability from the shores of India. And what does that banishment mean? It means universal love. It means translating into action the great message of the *Gita*: Treat the Brahmin and the bhangi alike if you would but know God. But how are they alike? A Brahmin is any day superior to the bhangi in learning, and how am I to treat both alike? The *Gita* says that you should treat them even as you would wish to be treated by them, or even as you would treat yourself. That hero and martyr translated this teaching into action in his own life and he has sanctified it, and sealed it with his blood. Let that blood purify us, and let it remove the last point of any isolation or aloofness, we may be harbouring against those brothers of ours whom in our arrogance we call 'untouchable'. They are not untouchables, we are untouchables. Let them have every attention and kindness that they deserve from us. * * * If a sum total of their virtues and vices and the privileges they are denied were to be made and compared with our virtues and vices and the privileges we enjoy and deny to them, I'm sure in God's books we should find our debit side far heavier than theirs. Let us then think no more of any single person on earth as untouchables.
>
> – D.G. Tendulkar: *Mahatma, op. cit.*, Vol. II, pp. 245-246.

As an incomparable spiritual artist, Gandhi portrays humanity in terms of love that has a certain sense of mystic detachment. He loves the distressed humanity not because he finds abnormalities but because he always yearns for good sense and sensibilities. He involves himself in the tremendous task of awakening the spiritual vision of man not because he wants to profess spiritualism but essentially because he believes in the greater emergence of spiritual vision among the marooned masses in drab politics and polluted social environment. 'A reformer with a revolutionary' as Rabindranath Tagore observes Gandhi as a man,[3] the mystic component of Gandhian spiritualism is the lesson of renunciation in the form of self-sacrifice which upholds him greater than the so called 'spiritual athletes' who find enjoyment in toying with primary and temporary components of bliss and happiness. His spiritualism aided and enriched by a greater mystic vision unfolds the glorious scene of a brighter tomorrow of humanity. As he serenely observes,

> It takes a fairly strenuous course of training to attain a mental state of non-violence. In daily life it has to be a course of discipline though one may not like it, like, for instance, the life of a soldier. But I agree that unless there is a hearty co-operation of the mind, the mere observance will be simply a mask, harmful both to the man himself and others. The perfect state is reached only when mind and body and speech are in proper co-ordination. But it is always a case of intense mental struggle.
>
> – M.K. Gandhi: *Young India*, October 1, 1931.

To spiritually consider non-violence an 'intense mental struggle' as Gandhi does all the time is to incorporate, practise and intensify the spirit of love. Love, as it were, replaces the sword of enmity in whatsoever form it might appear and allows the Kingdom of God to foster the inward spirit of man. Gandhi's own statement reveals his poignance of mystico-spiritual promise.

> Having flung aside the sword, there is nothing except the cup of love which I can offer to those who oppose me. It is by offering that cup that I expect to draw them close to me. I cannot think of permanent enmity between man and man and believing as I do in the theory of rebirth, in some other birth I shall be able to hug all humanity in friendly embrace.
>
> – M.K. Gandhi: *Young India*, April 2, 1931.

For a vision of the All Beautiful as a mystic efflorescence of spiritualism, Gandhi has, therefore, a firm belief within himself in the rebirth of man — the rebirth that is full of promise and perfection of humanity. This promise has been further substantiated by means of an adherence to non-possession as a mystic symbol of detachment – a total renunciation. With this mystic objective in view, an individual becomes truly spiritual in dedicating himself entirely to the service of humanity. Omnipresent as his soul is, why should it be allowed to be stifled in the cage-like body? Gandhi's mystic vision foresees the soul awaiting emancipation for Truth and so he thinks the body a barrier to the spiritual search for the All Beautiful. As he clearly observes,

> From the standpoint of Truth, the body too is a possession. It has been truly said that desire for enjoyment creates bodies for the soul. When this desire vanishes, there remains no further need for the body, and man is free from the vicious cycle of births and deaths. The soul is omnipresent; why should she care to be confined within the cage-like body, or do evil and even kill for the sake of that cage? We thus arrive at the ideal of total emancipation, and learn to use the body for the purpose of service as long as it exists, so much so that service, and not bread, becomes us the staff of life. We eat and drink, sleep and wake, for service alone. Such as attitude of mind brings us real happiness, and the beatific vision in the fulness of time.
>
> – M.K. Gandhi, *From Yeravda Mandir, op. cit.*, p. 37.

What Gandhi actually wants man to play his role as a man is to diminish himself to a cipher from all possible temptations – moral, social, intellectual or otherwise which might furnish the way to beyonding of himself. Like an ardent mystic he muses on the futility of man merged in matter of fullness and dwarfed in vain desires. The river of life, in the meantime, the river of spiritual profoundness, passes unnoticed. The flowers of mystic fragrance wither *sans* adoration. Gandhi's concept of spiritualism welcomes that mystic modesty of admitting the eternal nursing of the Supreme Spirit and rejuvenates the entire humanity with the promise of waking anew as Tagore does:

> On many an idle day have I grieved over lost times. But it is never lost, my lord. Thou hast taken every moment of my life in thine own hands.
>
> Hidden in the heart of things thou art nourishing seeds into sprouts, buds into blossoms, and ripening flowers into fruitfulness.
>
> I was tired and sleeping on my idle bed and imagined all work had ceased. In the morning I woke up and found my garden full with wonders of flowers.
>
> – Rabindranath Tagore: *Gitanjali*, (Song Offerings), *op. cit.*, No. LXXXI, p. 54.

Do we respond to the promise?

NOTES

1. The innermost essence of religion, apart from its outward machinery, is the search for God and the finding of God. All this has nothing to do with the realm of reason or its normal activities. Its sole legitimate sphere is to explain as best it can the truth, the experiences, the laws of our supra-physical and spiritual existence that has been the work of spiritual philosophy in the East, of theology in the West, a work of great importance at moments like the present. In the infrarational sphere, however, the reason might seem justified in its work and entitled to assume a superior role. But to root out the infrarational from religion or to purge religion of any elements necessary for its completeness because its forms are defective or obscure, without having the power to illuminate them from above or within or without replacing them by more luminous symbols, is not to purify but to pauperise. But the relations of the spirit and reason need not be always hostile or without any point of contact. What is impossible or absurd to the unaided reason, becomes real and right to reason lifted beyond itself by the power of the spirit and irradiated by its light.

— Sri Aurobindo: *The Human Cycle*, Abridgement by Sisirkumar Ghose, Sri Aurobindo Pathamandir, Calcutta. pp. 44-45.

2. The truth of humanity divinised in mystic consciousness blooms in celestial beauty in the following lines of Sri Aurobindo:

Rose of God, vermilion stain on the sapphires of heaven,
Rose of Bliss, fire-sweet, seven-tinged with the ecstasies seven
Leap up in our heart of homeland,
O miracle, O flame,
Passion flower of the Nameless, bud of the mystical Name.
Rose of God, great wisdom-bloom on the summits of being,
Rose of Light, immaculate core of the ultimate seeing
Live in the mind of our earthhood, golden Mystery flower,
Sun on the head of the Timeless, guest of the marvellous Hour.
Rose of God, demask forces of Infinity, red icon of light
Rose of Power, with thy diamond halo piercing the night
Ablaze in the will of the mortal, design the wonder of the plan,
Image of Immortality, outbreak of the Godhead in man.
Rose of God, smitten purple with the incarnate divine Desire,
Rose of Life, crowded with petals, colours' lyre
Transform the body of the mortal like a sweet and magical rhyme;
Bridge our earthhood and heavenhood, make deathless the children of time.
Rose of God, like a blush of rapture on Eternity's face,
Rose of Love, ruby depth of all being fire-passion of Grace
Arise from the heart of yearning that sobs in Nature's abyss;
Make earth the home of the Wonderful and life Beautiful kiss.

— Sri Aurobindo: "Rose of God", *Transformation and other Poems*, Sri Aurobindo Ashram, Pondicherry.

3. Gandhiji, like all dynamic personalities, needed a vast medium for the proper and harmonious expression of his creative will. This medium he developed for himself, when he assumed the tremendous responsibility of leading the whole country into freedom through countless social ditches and fences and unlimited dullness of barren politics. This endeavour has enriched and mellowed his personality and revealed what was truly significant in his genius. I have since learnt to understand him, as I would understand an artist, not by the theories and fantasies of the creed he may profess, but by that expression in his practice which gives evidence to the uniqueness of his mind. In that only true perspective, as I watch him I am amazed at the effectiveness of his humanity.

   An ascetic himself, he does not frown on the joys of others, but works for the enlivening of their existence day and night. He exalts poverty in his own life, but no man in India has striven more assiduously than he for the material welfare of his people. A reformer with the zeal of a revolutionary, he imposes severe restraints on the very passions he provokes. Something of an idolator and also an inconoclast, he leaves the old gods in their dusty niches of sanctity and simply lures the old worship to better and more humane purposes. Professing his adherence to the caste system, he launches his firmest attack against it where it keeps its strongest guards, and yet he has hardly suffered from popular disapprobation as would have been the case with a lesser man who would have much less power to be effective in his efforts.

* * * * * *

He advises his followers to hate evil without hating the evil-doer. It sounds an impossible precept, but he has made it as true as it can be made in his own life. I had once occasion to be present at an interview he gave a certain prominent politician who had been denounced by the official Congress Party as a deserter. Any other Congress leader would have assumed a repelling attitude, but Gandhiji was all graciousness and listened to him with patience and sympathy, without once giving him occasion to feel small. Here, I said to myself, is a truly great man, for he is greater than the party he belongs to, greater even than the creed he professes.

This then, seems to me to be the significant fact about Gandhiji. Great as he is as a politician, as an organizer, as a leader of men, as a moral reformer, he is greater than all these as a man, because none of these aspects and activities limits his humanity. They are rather inspired and sustained by it. Though an incorrigible idealist and given to referring all conduct to certain pet formulae of his own, he is essentially a lover of men and not of mere ideas; which makes him so cautious and conservative in his revolutionary schemes. If he proposes as experiment for society, has must first subject himself to its ordeal. If he calls for a sacrifice, he must first pay its price himself. While many socialists wait for all to be deprived of their privileges before they would part with theirs, this man first renounces before he ventures to make any claims on the renunciation of others.

There are patriots in India, as indeed among all peoples, who have sacrificed for their country as much as Gandhiji has done, and some who have had to suffer much worse penalties than he had ever to endure: even as in the religious sphere, there are ascetics in this country, compared to the rigours of whose practices Gandhiji's life is one of comparative ease. But these patriots are mere patriots and nothing more; and these ascetics are mere spiritual athletes, limited as men by their very virtues; while this man seems greater than his virtues, great as these are.

— Rabindranath Tagore: "Gandhi The Man", *The Visva-Bharati Quarterly*, Gandhi Number, Visva-Bharati, Santiniketan, Vol. 35, Nos. 1-4, May 1969-April 1970, pp. 29-32.

7

GANDHI AND VIVEKANANDA: Connoisseurs of Spiritual Consciousness

If spiritualism is the end in view of inward consciousness and the quest for excellence it cannot but infuse the spirit of Truth and service towards humanity. Truth as an invaluable spiritual essence is the first and last signal for spiritual consciousness. It is the mirror within every human being irrespective of caste, creed, colour, religion, race, nationality and innumerable other apparent points of dissociation. It is also the mirror that projects him before the world of marvels of humanity. The more one sees within the better is the avenue of inner consciousness that builds a bridge between what one is and what one should be to prove his unison with the All Beautiful.

How to prove one's unison with the All Beautiful? Is Truth enough as an entry to the Kingdom of the All Beautiful? Is it sufficient for energizing the inherent components of spiritual excellence? Or does it await something more for manifestation of spiritualism? The answers are varied and multi-dimensional. For, the vision of Truth is the outcome of experience little or great, in the light of humanism. Again, the vision of Truth is a fusion of experiences inward and outward. Admittedly, Truth to be Truth and a guide to encounter the All Beautiful greatly demands service in the diverse dimensions of promise and poignance. It also demands a certain sense of devotion which proves the fundamental objectives of spiritualism in the form of work as worship.

As eternal connoisseurs of spiritual consciousness both Mahatma Gandhi and Swami Vivekananda strive for spiritual excellence. The quest for which they dedicate themselves is a spiritual quest for the onward march — *charaiveti* — of mankind. It is a quest for that excellence which highlights Truth and service towards all under all trying situations. The inward journey for all round perfection, as Gandhi serenely feels, encompasses a preparation in undergoing *tapas* —

meditation — that purifies the soul for spiritual enlightenment in the form of self-suffering for the cause of humanity. Truth to be followed allows diverse directions and paths for man to unfold himself but then, Truth remains unchanged. As Gandhi characteristically unfolds,

> Does not God Himself appear to different individuals in different aspects? Still we know that He is One. But Truth is the right designation of God. Hence there is nothing wrong in everyone following Truth according to his rights. Indeed, it is his duty to do so. Then if there is a mistake on the part of anyone so following Truth, it will be automatically set right. For the quest of Truth involves *tapas* — self-suffering, sometimes even unto death. There can be no place in it for even trace of self-interest. In such selfless search for Truth nobody can lose his bearings for long. Directly he takes to the wrong path he stumbles, and is thus redirected to the right path.
>
> – M.K. Gandhi : *From Yeravda Mandir, op. cit.*, p.4.

Truly, Gandhi comes nearer to Swami Vivekananda who exposes and visualizes the Truth Ultimate as a poignant outcome of spiritualism that is developed in the Truth of Oneness:

> All the world has been preaching the God of virtue. I preach a God of virtue and a God of sin in one. Take Him if you dare — that is the one way to salvation; then alone will come to us the Truth Ultimate which comes from the idea of oneness. Then will be lost the idea that one is greater than another. The nearer we approach the law of freedom, the more we shall come under the Lord, and the troubles will vanish. Then we shall not differentiate the door of hell from the gate of heaven, nor differentiate between men and say, "I am greater than any being in the universe". Until we see nothing in the world but the Lord Himself, all these evils will beset us and we shall make all these distinctions; because it is only in the Lord, in the Spirit, that we are all one; and until we see God everywhere, this unity will not exist for us.
>
> – Swami Vivekananda : "What is Religion?", *The Complete Works of Swami Vivekananda*, Advaita Ashrama, Calcutta, 1989, Mayavati Memorial Edition, Vol. I, p. 339.

The great spiritual truth that Vivekananda wants to expose as above is that we are all one with the All Beautiful with all our differences in 'reflections'. His own delineation with this proposition by means of a characteristic simile makes it very thrilling and lively, simple and comprehensive :

> Two birds of beautiful plumage, inseparable companions, sat upon the same tree, one on the top and one below. The beautiful bird below was eating the fruits of the tree, sweet and bitter, one moment a sweet one and another a bitter. The moment he ate a bitter fruit, he was sorry, but after a while he ate another and when it too was bitter, he looked up and saw the other bird who ate neither the sweet nor the bitter, but was calm and majestic, immersed in his own glory. And then the poor lower bird forgot and went on eating the sweet and bitter fruits again, until at last he ate one that was extremely bitter; and then he stopped again and once more looked up at the glorious bird above. Then he came nearer and nearer to the other bird; and when he had come near enough, rays of light shone upon him and enveloped him, and he saw he was transformed into the higher bird. He became calm, majestic, free, and found that there had been but one bird all the time on the tree. The lower bird was but the reflection of the one above. So we have in reality one with the Lord, but the reflection makes us seem many, as when the one sun reflects in a million dew-drops and seems a million tiny suns. The reflection must vanish if we are to identify ourselves with our real nature which is divine. The universe itself can never be the limit of our satisfaction. That is why the miser gathers more and more money, that is why the robber robs, the sinner sins, that is why you are learning philosophy. All have one purpose. There is no other purpose in life, save to reach this freedom. Consciously or unconsciously, we are all striving for perfection.
>
> – *Ibid.*, pp. 339-340.

The fundamental lesson of spiritualism that Gandhi undertakes at the time of his first sojourn in South Africa is the lesson of this Ultimate Truth that has inspired him to go through three principal books. The first one is, of course, Swami Vivekananda's *Raja Yoga*, the other two being Patanjali's Yoga Sutras and the Gita. In fact, the two concepts that greatly encourage him to be nearer to spiritual fulfilment are *aparigraha* (non-possession) and *samabhavana* (equability). A change of heart coupled with a change of attitude towards the well-being of all, makes spiritualism living and dynamic. Gandhi strives to disseminate this living and dynamic concept of spiritualism : 'to see Him in His creation and be one with it'. As he explicitly observes,

> Man's ultimate aim is the realization of God, and all his activities, social, political, religious, have to be guided by the ultimate aim of the vision of God. The immediate service of all human beings becomes a necessary part of the endeavour, simply because the only way to find God is to see Him in His creation and be one with it. This can only be done by service of all. I am a part and parcel of the whole, and I cannot find Him apart from the rest of humanity. My countrymen are my nearest neighbours. They have become so helpless so resourceless, so inert that I must concentrate myself on serving them.
>
> — M.K. Gandhi : *Harijan*, August 29, 1936.

The concept of *daridranarayana*, the poor as an embodiment of God, is the living concept of Gandhian spiritualism which is exactly a replica of Vivekananda's clarion call to serve the distressed humanity in order to serve the *Narayana*, the living God incarnate in man. In this connection, one might recall Gandhi's address to the merchants of Sri Lanka on November 13, 1927 :

> I appeal to you to open out your purses for Daridranarayana. I can conceive of no better investment for the wealthy Indians, whether in India or outside, and let not your generosity end with merely giving money. If you will establish a living bond with these dumb millions, you must wear khaddar which is produced by their sacred hands. * * * You, as merchants in this hospitable land, are expected to behave towards the indigenous population in an exemplary and honest manner. By your conduct will be judged the conduct of the millions of India. * * * Let possession of wealth not render us giddy. It must carry with it a greater sense of responsibility, if it is to be a blessing to the possessor and those in whose midst it is earned.
>
> — D.G. Tendulkar : *Mahatma, op. cit.*, Vol. II, p. 291.

To visualize the Living God as one and the same in different ways and through different religious principles and principles is the poignance of spiritualism which Gandhi always emphasizes in course of his exposition of God as a great spiritual force. In fact, he always stresses on that essence of spiritualism which would turn man to realize religion as a great inward force that can only be achieved in course of our serene and pure leading of lives, As he frankly observes,

> I claim to be a man of faith and prayer, and even if I were out to pieces, I trust God would give me the strength not to deny Him and to assert that He is. The Muslim says, He is and there is no one else. The Christian says the same thing and so the Hindus, and if I may say so, even the Buddhist says the same thing, if in different words. Thus though we may utter the same words, they have not same meaning for us all. And hence I say that we do not need to proselytize or do *shuddhi* or *tabligh* through our speech or writing. We can really do it with our lives. Let them be open books for all to study.
>
> — *Ibid.*, p. 294.

Vivekananda makes a firmer appeal, a more forceful beckoning for awakening of the inner truth than Gandhi and upholds Truth as the essence of all spiritualism, self-purification and knowledge. It is the education of all education and the religion of all religions. The spirituality of manliness that he wants everyone to recognize, practise and perform in the promise of poignance is Truth. As he strongly observes,

> What we want is strength, so believe in yourselves. * * * Make your nerves strong. What we want is muscles of iron and nerves of steel. We have wept long enough; no more weeping but stand on your feet and be men. It is a man-making religion that we want. It is man-making theories that we want. It is man-making education all around that we want. And here is the test of truth : anything that makes you weak, physical, intellectually, and spiritually, reject as poison, there is no life in it, it cannot be true. Truth is strengthening, Truth is purity, Truth is all-knowledge.
>
> — Swami Vivekananda : "My Plan of Campaign", *The Complete Works of Swami Vivekananda*, 1960 Edition, Vol. III, pp. 224-228.

Elsewhere, in explaining spirituality from the practical points of view, Vivekananda shows how the spiritual man bereft of self-glory and self-satisfaction, and fired with the spirit of patriotism becomes a glowing disciple of the All Beautiful :

> The *Tapas* and the other hard *Yogas* that were practised in other *Yugas* do not work now. What is needed in this *Yuga* is giving, helping others. What is meant by *Dana*. The highest of gifts is the giving of spiritual knowledge, the next is the giving of secular knowledge, and the next is the saving of life, the last is giving food and drink. He who gives spiritual knowledge, saves the soul from many and many a birth. He who gives secular knowledge opens the eyes of human beings towards spiritual knowledge, and far below these rank all other gifts, even the saving of life. There it is necessary that you learn this and note that all other kinds of work are of much less value than that of imparting spiritual knowledge. The highest and greatest help is that given in the dissemination of spiritual knowledge. There is an eternal fountain of spirituality in our scriptures, and nowhere on earth, except in this land of renunciation, do we find such noble examples of practical spirituality. I have had a little experience of the world. Believe me there is much talking in other lands; but the practical man of religion, who has carried it into his life, is here and here alone. Talking is not religion; parrots may talk, machine may talk now-a-days. But show me the life of renunciation, of spirituality, of self-suffering of love infinite. This kind of life indicates a spiritual man. With such ideas and such noble practical examples in our country, it would be a great pity if the treasures in the brains and hearts of all these great *Yogis* were not brought out to become the common property of everyone, rich and poor, high and low; not only in India, but they must be thrown broadcast all over the world. This is one of our greatest duties, and you will find that the more you work to help others, the more you help yourself. The one vital duty incumbent on you, if you really love your religion, if you really love your country, is that you must struggle hard to be up and doing, with this one great idea of bringing out the treasures from your closed books and delivering them over to their rightful heirs.
>
> —*Ibid.*, pp. 133-134

To bring out the inner truth for the efflorescence of 'man' in man is to be in the true spirit of the blooming of the Lotus Land of Purity and Consciousness. The search for the All Serene is always a search for the essence of religion which is Truth. That Truth in each man suffering and toiling in void necessitates a release from all bondage of apathy and ignorance. A deep sense of faith nursed in the Truth of regeneration of mankind opens out a new vista of spiritualism of which man alone is proud and with which he is eternally blessed by the All Beautiful. In this connection, Gandhi's note of optimism is significant :

> There are those who are struck with doubt and despair. For them there is the name of God. It is God's covenant that whoever goes to Him in weakness and helplessness, him He will make strong. 'When I am weak, then I am strong'. As the Poet Surdas has sung, Rama is the strength of the weak. This strength is not to be obtained by taking up arms or by similar means. It is to be had by throwing oneself on His name. Rama is the synonym of God. You may say God or Allah or whatever other name you like, but the moment you trust naught but Him, you are strong, all disappointment disappears. The hymn alludes to the story of the Lord of elephants who was in the jaws of a crocodile and who had been all but drowned in water. There was only the tip of his trunk left above water when he invoked God's name and was saved. No doubt it is an allegory. But it conceals a truth. Over and over again in my life have I found it. Even in darkest despair, when there seems no helper and no comfort in the wide wide world, His name inspires us with strength and puts all doubts and despair to flight. The sky may be overcast today with clouds, but a fervent prayer to him is enough to dispel them. It is because of prayer that I have known no disappointment. * * * Let us pray that He may cleanse our hearts of pettiness, meanness and deceit, and He will surely answer our prayers.
>
> — M.K. Gandhi : *Harijan*, June 1, 1935.

Admittedly, like Vivekananda, Gandhi also conceives education as a man-making and character building process which he believes to be an essence of spiritualism. Sticktoitiveness to Truth under all circumstances by means of sincere action and devotion is, as he affirms, all that is needed through prayer. Explaining to the pupils the quest for Truth by means of prayer as 'the alpha and omega of all education', he remarks :

> There are several things in this prayer which are worthy of your note, but I want to draw your attention to that particular portion of it which pledged the reciter to adherence to truth in speech and action under all circumstances and at all times. One mantra means Lead me from Untruth to Truth, from Darkness to Light, from Death to Immortality. Similarly, the Islamic prayer * * * is an outpouring of the soul, for light and for being guided on the straight path of truth and righteousness.
>
> — D.G. Tendulkar : *Mahatma, op. cit.*, Vol. VI, pp. 296-297.

To enthrone God in the heart all the time by knowing, thinking and doing good to humanity is the truest lesson of Gandhian spiritualism that echoes in fullest measure the spiritual vision of Vivekananda. Accordingly, Gandhi needs education to play its vital role to clean the mind and body of a learner who might significantly be of use to the neighbours and the society. Truth, then, comes out as a living force in every learner who purifies his spirit of contemplation through action in being one of the members of the Great Family of Man. That Gandhi pins a great deal of stress on cleanliness through education has its roots on the belief in God as Truth. As he elucidates his view-points on New Education :

> Cleanliness of the mind and body is the first step in education. Prayer does for the purification of the mind, what the bucket and the broom do for the cleaning up our physical surroundings. And that is why we always commence our proceedings with prayer. No matter whether the prayer we recite is the Hindu prayer or the Muslim or the Parsi, its function is essentially the same, namely, purification of the heart. God has innumerable name, but the most beautiful and suitable, in my opinion is Truth. Let Truth, therefore, rule every action of our life, be it ever so insignificant. Let every morsel of food that we eat be sanctified with His name and consecrated to His service. Not only will it make our bodies and minds healthy and clean, the inner cleanliness will be reflected in our surroundings also. * * *

> As with the individual so with the society. A village is but a group of individuals, and the world, as I see it, is one vast village, and mankind one family. The various functions in the human body have been parallel in the corporate life of society. What I have said about inner and outer cleanliness of the individual, therefore, applies to the whole society.
>
> In the mighty world, man considered as an animal occupies but an insignificant place. Physically, he is a contemptible worm. But God has endowed him with intellect and faculty of discrimination between good and evil. If we use this faculty to know God, we become a power for good. Abuse of that talent converts us into an instrument of evil, so that we become like scourge and a plague and fill this earth with strife and bloodshed and unhappiness and misery.
>
> The struggle between the forces of good and evil is ceaseless and eternal. The former have truth and ahimsa as weapon against the latter's falsehood, violence and brute force. There is nothing more potent in the universe than God's name. If we enthrone Him in our hearts and keep Him there always, then we shall know no fear and lay for ourselves rich treasure in life.
>
> *Ibid.*, pp. 297-298.

A seeker of God as the embodiment of Truth in the true spiritual perspective finds no difference between the God of a Christian and that of a Hindu or a Muslim or a Buddhist or a Sikh as the case may be. For, true religion is always a unison of universal goodness and faith for the cause of human excellence. Gandhi emphasizes on that very human excellence where the concept of God as an embodiment of human excellence in the form of Truth guides and directs an individual to be worthy of humanity. Truth as the spiritual vision of God makes God more endearing and acceptable even with differences of approach to diverse religious faith. For, Truth is all existent and all-pervading irrespective of any course of action whatsoever. Gandhi as a spiritual introspector goes a step further in highlighting Truth as Love in the ultimate vision of God, the embodiment of Truth, as Love. In his own words,

> We believe — and I think it is the truth — that God has many names as there are creatures and, therefore, we also say that God

is nameless and since God has many forms we also consider Him formless, and since He speaks to us through many tongues we consider Him to be speechless and so on. And when I came to study Islam I found that Islam too had many names for God. I would say with those who say God is Love, God is Love. But deep down in me I used to say that though God may be God, God is Truth above all. If it is possible for the human tongue to give the fullest description, I have come to the conclusion that for myself God is Truth. But two years ago, I went a step further and said Truth is God. You will see the fine distinction between the two statements, *viz.*, that God is Truth and Truth is God. And I came to that conclusion after a continuous and relentless search after Truth which began nearly fifty years ago. I then found that the nearest approach to Truth was through love. But I also found that love has many meanings in the English language at least and that human love in the sense of passion could become a degrading thing also. I found, too, that love in the sense of *ahimsa* had only a limited member of votaries in the world. But I never found a double meaning in connection with truth and not even the atheists had demurred to the necessity or power of truth. But in their passion for discovering truth the atheists have not hesitated to deny the very existence of God — from their own point of view rightly. And it was because of this reasoning that I saw that rather than say God is Truth I should say Truth is God. * * * Not that scientists very often do not commit cruelties in the name of truth. I know how in the name of truth and science inhuman cruelties are perpetrated on animals when men perform vivisection. There are thus a number of difficulties in the way, no matter how you describe God. But the human mind is a limited thing, and you have to labour under limitations when you think of a being or entity who is beyond the power of man to grasp. And then we have another thing in Hindu philosophy, *viz.*, God alone is and nothing else exists, and the same truth you find emphasized and exemplified in the *Kalema* of Islam. There you find it clearly stated — that God alone is and nothing else exists. In fact, the Sanskrit word for Truth is a word which literally means that which exists — *Sat*. For these and several other reasons that I can give you I have come to the conclusion that the definition — Truth is God — gives me the greatest satisfaction. And when you want to find Truth as God the only inevitable means is Love, i.e. non-violence, and since I believe that ultimatelv means and end are convertible terms, I should not hesitate to say that God is Love.

— M.K. Gandhi : *Young India*, December 31, 1931.

Love as the touchstone of spiritual emancipation leads, as Gandhi more than once emphasizes, to the ultimate realization of Truth which is God. In Vivekananda, the same sense of Love as the revelation of God manifests in the practical lesson of service towards mankind. This is the only religion to be followed. This is true spiritualism for, this means awareness to the all-round existence of God who lives in all human beings. In a letter to Alasinga Perumal, Swami Vivekananda writes,

> I am a *Tyagi* (detached) monk. I only want one thing. I do not believe in a God or religion which cannot wipe the widow's tears or bring a piece of bread to the orphan's mouth. However sublime be the theories, however well-spun be the philosophy — I do not call it religion so long as it is confined to books and dogmas. The eye is in the forehead and not in the back. Move onward and carry into practice that which you are proud to call your religion, and God bless you!
>
> Look not at me, look to yourselves. I am happy to have been the occasion of rousing an enthusiasm. Take advantage of it, float along with it, and everything will come right. Love never fails, my son; today or tomorrow or ages after, truth will conquer. Love shall win the victory. Do you love your fellowmen.? Where should you go to seek for God — are not all the poor, the miserable, the weak, Gods? Why not worship them first? Why go to dig a well on the shores of the Ganga? Believe in the omnipotent power of love. Who cares for these tinsel puffs of name? I never keep watch of what the newspapers are saying. Have you love? — You are omnipotent. Are you perfectly unselfish? If so, you are irresistible. It is character that pays everywhere. It is the Lord who protects His children in the depths of the sea. * * * My son, I believe in God, and I believe in man. I believe in helping the miserable. I believe in going even to hell to save others.

—Swami Vivekananda : "Epistles", *The Complete Works of Swami Vivekananda*, Màyavati Memorial Edition, Advaita Ashrama, Calcutta 1989, Vol. V, pp. 50-52.

To seek the All Beautiful by evading humanity is to seek in vain. The core of spiritualism, as Vivekananda clearly remarks is being and becoming. It is the total orientation of soul for service towards all. That true religion is true realization of the self for the well-being of everyone is the first lesson of *Jnana-Yoga* which teaches the lesson of Thou art That — *tat tamhasi*. It is the lesson to understand the inward divinity in each individual. Elucidating the teachings of the *Jnana-Yoga*, Vivekananda unfolds the spiritual vision of God in a very characteristic manner :

> It (*Jnana-Yoga*) tells man that he is essentially divine. It shows to mankind the real unity of being, and that each one of us is the Lord God Himself, manifested on earth. All of us, from the lowest worm that crawls under our feet to the highest beings to whom we look up with wonder and awe — all are manifestation of the same Lord.
>
> — Swami Vivekananda : "The Ideal of a Universal Religion", *The Complete Works of Swami Vivekananda, op. cit.*, Vol. II, p. 396.

With such a spiritual vision of God as above, Vivekananda explains the concept of religion not as a mere doctrine but as realisation of being and becoming:

> We have to reason the thoughts out, impress them on our minds, and we have to meditate on them, realise them, until at last they become our whole life. No longer will religion remain a bundle of ideas or theories, nor an intellectual assent; it will enter into our very self. By means of intellectual assent we may today ascribe to many foolish things, and change our minds altogether tomorrow. But true religion never changes. Religion is realisation; not talk, nor doctrine, nor theories, however beautiful they may be. It is being and becoming, not hearing or acknowledgeing; it is the whole soul becoming changed into what it believes. That is religion.
>
> —*Ibid.*, p. 396.

Gandhi also makes a fine analysis of religion in terms of realisation. He thinks that true religion is always a search for Truth, and as such, it cannot but encompass the whole of mankind to evolve in spiritual excellence. This identification with the whole of mankind opens out the newer avenues of spiritual emancipation. Religion that ends in mere theorisation fails to appeal the spirit within, — 'the inner voice' in every human being — but when it is oriented and practised in activities related to the well-being of humanity, it becomes living, dynamic, spiritual and serene. Gandhi's frank observation makes religion very appealing towards realisation of humanity in terms of Truth that acts in living faith :

> It is faith that steers us through stormy seas, faith that moves mountains and faith that jumps across the ocean. That faith is nothing but a living wide-awake consciousness of God within. He who has achieved that faith wants nothing. Bodily diseased, he is spiritually healthy; physically poor, he rolls in spiritual riches.
>
> — R.K. Prabhu, & U.R. Rao (Compiled) : *op. cit.*, p. 80.

Viewing Truth as God, Gandhi signifies the poignance of his spiritual vision in the same fashion as Vivekananda does and goes on experimenting upon Truth as the best process of self-realization for unison with the All Serene by means of evolution in action[1]. The consequences are to be assessed by the Great Power and so one needs only to seek for Truth in action and action alone. As he says,

> All that we know is that one should do one's duty and leave the result in the hands of God. Man is supposed to be the master of his own destiny, but it is only partly true. He can make his own destiny only in so far as he is allowed by the Great Power which over-rides all our intentions, all our plans and carries out His own plans. I call that Power not by the name of *Allah, Khuda* or God but Truth. The whole truth is embodied only within the heart of that Great Power — Truth.

— Pyarelal : *Mahatma Gandhi : The Last Phase, op. cit.,* Vol. II, p. 91.

Gandhi, of course, feels confident of the inner voice of service towards humanity and for this he thinks the value of life less important than death because if death ameliorates the sufferings of mankind the inner spirit of man achieves the coveted victory. He, therefore, surrenders to the Great Power to enjoy the worth of life in death. Referring to his fast unto death for the cause of the despised Harijans on May 5, 1933, he humbly submits his adherence to the call from within — the spiritual call for eternal conscience of humanity — which, as he strongly feels is prompted by the spirits of Ramakrishna and Vivekananda:

> My claim to hear the voice of God is not new. Unfortunately, there is no way of proving my claim except through results. God will not be God, if He allowed Himself to be the object proof by His creatures. But He does give His willing slave the power to pass through the fiercest of ordeals. I have been a willing slave to this most exacting Master for more than half a century. His voice has been increasingly audible as the years have rolled by. He has never forsaken me in my darkest hour. He has saved me often against myself and left me not a vestige of independence. The greater the surrender to Him the greater has been my joy. I, therefore, feel confident that these kindest of friends will recognise the correctness of the action I am about to take and this whether I live or die. God's ways are inscrutable. And who knows, He may not want my death during the fast to be more fruitful of beneficent results than my life?
>
> Surely, it is depressing to think that man's ability to serve dies with the dissolution of the body, which for the moment he is inhabiting. Who doubts that the spirits of Ramakrishna and Vivekananda, Dayanand and Ramatirth, are working today among our midst? It may be that they are more potent today than when they were in our midst in flesh. It is not true that what good men do is oft buried with them. We burn the evil men do, with their mortal remains. We treasure the memory of the good they do, and distance magnifies it. And why should exaggerated importance be given to the services of a single person, however good or able he may be?
>
> — M.K. Gandhi : *Harijan*, 5, 1933.

Elsewhere, Gandhi makes almost the same exposition in feeling the 'divine music of God' as the inner spirit of consciousness within every human being. He also refers that unless we feel so and have 'a living immovable faith', any endeavour on our part to achieve spiritual height is bound to be a failure. As he characteristically unfolds,

> Not all the achievements of physical sciences put together can compare with that which gives us a living faith in God. Those who do not want to believe in the existence of God do not believe in the existence of anything apart from the body. Such a belief is held to be unnecessary for the progress of humanity. For such persons the weightiest argument in proof of the existence of soul or God is of no avail. You cannot make a person who has stuffed his ears, listen to, much less appreciate, the finest music. Even so can you not convince those about existence of a living God who do not want the conviction?
>
> Fortunately, the vast majority of people do have a living faith in a living God. They cannot, will not, argue about it. For them, "It is". Are all the scriptures of the world old women's tales of superstition? Is the testimony of the Rishis, the Prophets to be rejected? Is the testimony of Chaitanya, Ramakrishna Paramahamsa, Tukaram, Dayananda, Ramdas, Nanak, Kabir, Tulsidas of no value? What about Rammohan Roy, Devendranath Tagore, Vivekananda — all modern men as well educated as the tallest among the living ones? I omit the living witnesses whose evidence would be considered unimpeachable. This belief in God has to be based on faith which transcends reason. Indeed even the so-called realization has at bottom an element of faith without which it cannot be sustained. In the very nature of things it must be so. Who can transgress the limitations of his being? I hold that complete realization is impossible in this embodied life. Nor is it necessary. A living immovable faith is all that is required for reaching the full spiritual height attainable by human beings. God is not outside this earthly case of ours. Therefore exterior proof is not of much avail, if any at all. We must ever fail to perceive Him through the senses, because He is beyond them. We can feel Him, if we will but withdraw ourselves from the senses. The divine music is incessantly going on within ourselves, but the loud senses drown the delicate music which is unlike and infinitely superior to anything we perceive or hear within our senses.
>
> — M.K. Gandhi : *Harijan*, June 13, 1936.

The divine music of the All Serene, as Gandhi strongly advocates, comes close to the rich spiritual muse of Swami Vivekananda who realizes and emphasizes upon man as the living embodiment of God. The curse of ignorance is, as the latter time and again remarks, the curse of humanity. It differentiates between man and God, between the spirit in man and the Spirit Eternal which is indeed the purified, practised and poignant spirit of man. The divine muse of the Spirit Eternal is, as Vivekananda also strongly advocates, for those who are willing to undergo diverse tests and pitfalls of life, live for an ideal to be purified by means of lessons learnt through manifold experiences in order to have spiritual perfection. His serene exposition is:

> If you want to be a *Yogi,* you must be free, and place yourself in circumstances where you are alone and free from all anxiety. He who desires a comfortable and nice life and at the same time wants to realise the Self is like the fool who, wanting to cross the river, caught hold of a crocodile, mistaking it for a log of wood. "Seek ye first the kingdom of God, and everything shall be added unto you" This is the one great duty, this is renunciation. Live for an ideal, and leave no place in the mind for anything else. Let us put forth all our energies to acquire that which never fails — our spiritual perfection. If we have true yearning for realisation, we must struggle, and through struggle growth will come. We shall make mistakes, but they may be angels unawares.
>
> The greatest help to spiritual life is meditation (*Dhyana*). In meditation we divest ourselves of all material conditions and feel our divine nature. We do not depend upon any external help in meditation. The touch of the soul can paint the brightest colour even in the dingiest places; it casts a fragrance over the vilest thing : it can make the wicked divine — and all enmity, all selfishness is effaced. The less the thought of the body, the better. For it is the body that drags us down. It is attachment, identification, which makes us miserable. That is the secret : To think that I am the spirit and not the body, and that the whole of this universe with all its relations, with all its good and all its evil, is but as a series of paintings — scenes on a canvas — of which I am a witness.

— Swami Vivekananda : *The Complete Works of Swami Vivekananda, op. cit.*, Vol. II, 1989, pp. 36-37.

As an undaunted spiritual connoisseur, Vivekananda goes deeper into the heartland of humanity and places man as the Great Light for which every man yearns. True faith is this true realisation of God within every man the Self Bible or the Self Christ. The realisation of the Infinite in the midst of every man is the be all and end all of spiritualism. The reflection is there — the inward reflection, so to say, in every man but it is the realisation of manhood that changes the materialistic approach to life. Life as it is, is *sans* the spiritual blessings that we greatly deserve. The goal remains far away. What is fulfilment by means of purification in action as Gandhi believes in the realisation of true religion is also the same in case of Vivekananda who categorically believes in the realisation of God in ourselves and ourselves alone. How to have such truth? How to have such spiritual realization? Vivekananda shows a genuine way :

> I am in the sun, the moon, and the stars. I am with God and I am in all the gods. I worship my Self.
>
> There is another side to it. I have kept it in reserve. I am the man that is going to be hanged. I am all the wicked. I am getting punished in hells. That (also) is fun. This is the goal of philosophy (to know that I am the Infinite). Aims, motives, purposes and duties live in the background. * * *
>
> This truth is first to be listened to, then to be thought about. Reason, argue it by all manner of means. The enlightened know no more than that. Know it for certain that you are in everything. That is why you should not hurt anybody, because in hurting them you hurt yourself. * * *
>
> I am One, alone, through all eternity. Whom shall I fear? It is all my Self. This is continuously to be meditated upon. Through that comes realisation. It is through realisation that you become a (blessing) to others * * *
>
> If there is this truth, if there is God, it must be within us. * * * (I must be able to say,) "I have seen Him with my eyes". Otherwise I have no religion. Beliefs, doctrines, sermons do not make religion. It is realisation, perception of God (which alone is religion). What is the glory of all these men whom the world worships? God was no more a doctrine (for them. Did they believe) because their grandfather believed it? No. It was the realisation of the Infinite, higher than their own bodies, minds and everything. This world is real inasmuch as it contains a little bit (of) the

> reflection of that God. We love the good man because in his face shines the reflection a little more. We must catch it ourselves. There is no other way.
>
> That is the goal. Struggle for it! Have your own Bible. Have your own Christ. Otherwise you are not religious. Do not talk religion. Men talk and talk. "Some of them, steeped in darkness, in the pride of their hearts think that they have the light. And not only (that), they offer to take others upon their shoulders and both fall into the pit". * * *
>
> In the midst of the manifold, he who sees that One; in the midst of this infinite death, he who sees that one life, in the midst of the manifold, he who sees that which never changes in his own soul — unto him belongs eternal peace.
>
> *Ibid.*, pp. 472-74.

The transcendental nature of religion that Gandhi approaches towards realization of the All Serene in action is the outcome of his broad spiritual vision and this makes the same appeal as that which we achieve by means of the spiritual vision of Vivekananda as revealed above. As Gandhi clearly observes,

> I have no special revelation of God's will. My firm belief is that He reveals Himself daily to every human being, but we shut our ears to the 'still small voice'. We shut our eyes to the 'pillar of fire' in front of us.
>
> — R.K. Prabhu & U.R. Rao (Compiled) : *op. cit.*, p. 23.

For an individual to hear the 'still small voice' within and visualize the 'pillar of fire', what Gandhi wants is to be spiritual primarily from three directions : first, to stick to truth under any circumstances, secondly, to be bold enough to meet any eventuality for the cause of truth, and thirdly, to be enkindled with the spirit of austerity and charity. The real battle of mankind is always within. It is the battle of betterment of conscience — a preparation to be hallowed with the Light Eternal. It is more arduous to carry the burden of being and becoming than that of a heavy militia nourishing aggression and greed. In the poignant words of Gandhi,

> Ours will only then be a truly spiritual nation when we shall show more truth than gold, greater fearlessness than pomp of power and wealth, greater charity than love of self. If we will but clean our houses, our palaces and temples of the attributes of wealth and show in them the attributes of morality, one can offer battle to any combination of hostile forces, without having to carry the burden of a heavy militia.
>
> — D.G. Tendulkar : *Mahatma, op. cit.*, Vol. I, pp. 241-242

A perfect purity of character nursed in a mind pure and serene is as Gandhi strongly advocates, the touchstone of spiritualism. It is that spiritual insight which allows one to mingle oneself with one and all irrespective of caste and creed. It is that revolution which brings about the most desirable triple purity of thought, word and deed. Gandhi's own spiritual vision is exposed as follows :

> What we need is boundless faith backed by perfect purity of character. An impure mind and a religious spirit go ill together. By purity of character is here meant truth, love and chastity in thought, world and deed. If we have not these we shall neither move the castemen nor the Harijans. If we have not this triple purity, not only shall we fail to steal the hearts of either, but by our failure we shall discredit not merely ourselves but the great cause we represent.
>
> — M.K. Gandhi : *Harijan*, August 19, 1933.

What Gandhi says above in connection with purity of character echoes the internal purification as exposed by Swami Vivekananda for spiritual efflorescence. The latter identifies it as the component of true *bhakti* — which, in the end makes a unison of God in everything and everything in God. Man, then, is merged in the spiritual vision of Oneness. As Vivekananda elucidates,

> Do we always speak the truth? What happens is often this. People go to the house of a rich person for some business of their own and flatter him by calling him benefactor of the poor and so forth, even though that man may cut the throat of a poor man coming to his house. What is this? Nothing but falsehood. And it is this that

> pollutes the mind. It is therefore, truly said that whatever a man says who has purified his inner self for twelve years without entertaining a single vicious idea during that period is sure to come true. This is the power of truth, and one who has cleaned both the inner and the outer self is alone capable of Bhakti. But the beauty is that Bhakti itself cleanses the mind to a great extent. * * *
>
> It is not Bhakti if we worship God with the desire for a son; it is not Bhakti if we worship with the desire to be rich; it is not Bhakti even if we have a desire for heaven; it is not Bhakti if a man worships with the desire of being saved from the tortures of hell. Bhakti is not the outcome of fear or greediness. He is the true Bhagavata who says, "O God, I do not want a beautiful wife, I do not want knowledge or salvation. Let me be born and die hundreds of times. What I want is that I should be ever engaged in Thy service". It is at this stage — and when a man sees God in everything, and everything in God — that he attains perfect Bhakti. It is then that he sees Vishnu incarnated in everything from the microbe to Brahma, and it is then that he sees God manifesting Himself in everything, it is then that he feels that there is nothing without God, and it is then and then alone that thinking himself to be the most insignificant of all beings he worships God with the true spirit of a Bhakta. He then leaves Tirthas and external forms of worship far behind him, he sees every man to be the most perfect temple.
>
> — Swami Vivekananda : *op. cit.,*, Vol. III, pp. 361-363.

Vivekananda identifies God as an embodiment of Love, He personified the God of Love from the spiritual point of view. Therefore, what is worship to an ordinary person is the beginning or practice of spiritualism according to Vivekananda. He holds it as a form of worship which is external and love ends in the identification of God as a creator and preserver. This external worship is of no value unless it is purified in the vision of God as Love Incarnate. This, then, is true spiritualism which can be hallowed in *Bhakti.* As Vivekananda serenely observes,

> God is love personified. He is apparent in everything. Everybody is being drawn to Him whether he knows it or not. When a woman loves her husband, he does not understand that it is the

> divine in her husband that is the great attractive power. The God of Love is the one thing to be worshipped. So long as we think of Him only as the Creator and Preserver, we can offer Him external worship, but when we get beyond all that and think Him to be Love Incarnate, seeing Him in all things and all things in Him, it is then that supreme Bhakti is attained.
>
> —*Ibid.*, p. 365.

God as Love Incarnate is the eternal source of Bhakti to Gandhi, too. He spiritualizes *Bhakti* in terms of selfless devotion to service and detachment from consequences whatsoever. Renunciation of the fruit of action as suggested by him in his discourse of the *Gita* is the surest way to spiritual efflorescence. As he observes in his 'note' on the ninth chapter of the *Gita*,

> We learn from this chapter that devotion (*bhakti*) means attachment (*asakti*) to God. This is the royal road to the cultivation of the selfless spirit. Therefore we are told at the beginning that devotion is the sovereign yoga and is easy to practise. It is easy to practise if it takes hold of our heart, but hard going if it does not. Hence it has been described as something for which we have to offer our life itself as the price. But he who has plunged into it enjoys perfect bliss though it scares the mere spectator. Sudhanya was laughing as he lay in the boiling oil while the bystanders were seized with terror and anxiety. The untouchable Nanda is said to have danced as he was tried by the ordeal of fire. We need not bother whether or not these are true stories. But the fact is that a man reaches such a state of calmness and imperturbability when he is absorbed in something or other. He forgets himself. But who would set his heart on anything except God? 'Do not prefer the bitter nimba to sugar-cane or the glowworm to the sun and the moon'. The ninth chapter thus shows that renunciation of the fruit of action is impossible without devotion (*bhakti*).
>
> — M.K. Gandhi : "Discourse on Gita", *In Search of the Supreme*, Navajivan Publishing House, Ahmedabad, 1962, Vol. III, pp. 253-254.

How, as a spiritual connoisseur, does Gandhi visualize devotion or *Bhakti* as a form of renunciation of the fruit of action? What should be the strategies for a true devotee as a spiritual effortee? Gandhi's exposition is significant :

> The devotee will not draw up schemes of future expansion. For example, if a merchant who deals in cloth now has any plans of selling firewood as well in the future, or if he, having one shop only, thinks of opening five more shops, that would be *arambha* (undertaking) on his past, and the devotee will have none of it. This principle is applicable to service of the nation as well. For instance, a worker in the *khadi* department today will not take up cow-keeping tomorrow, agriculture the day after and medical aid on the fourth day. He will do his best in whatever has come to him. When I am free from egoism, nothing remains for me to do. * * * A devotee's every activity is planned by God. It comes to him as in the natural course of things. He therefore rests content with, this 'that or anything else' (*yena kenochit*). This is the meaning of 'renouncing all undertakings'. The devotee does not cease to work; indeed he is nothing if not a worker. He only ceases to think needless thoughts about his work. It is these that he has to renounce.
>
> *Idamadya maya lavdhang imang prapsye manoratham* (This has been acquired by me today; that purpose I shall gain tomorrow). — this is the opposite of 'renouncing undertakings'.
>
> —*Ibid*., p. 259.

Renunciation of everything for the cause of the All Beautiful is the keynote of Gandhian spiritualism. The sense of devotion or *bhakti* that he upholds is the sense of all-round purification in thought, word and deed. This sense of devotion actually spells out the true concept of God and religion, because it leads to self-consciousness and self-realization. In Vivekananda, too, the concept of religion in the final analysis of spiritualism is : what you *are* and what you have *realised*. With this realization of the self man marches ahead by making a unison between his personal God and *Brahman*, the Absolute so that he might avert his little self and endear the Supreme Self. While spelling out spiritualism in terms of the diverse aspects of devotion, Vivekananda observes with characteristic simplicity and poignance of thought :

Close your eyes and think what He is. What do you find? Either you are thinking, in bringing the idea of omnipresence in your mind, of the sea, or the blue sky, or an expanse of meadow, or such things as you have seen in your life. If that is so, you do not mean anything by omnipresent God; it has no meaning at all to you. So with every other attribute of God. What idea have we of omnipresence or omniscience? We have none. Religion is realising, and I shall call you a worshipper of God when you have become able to realise the Idea. Before that it is the spelling of words and no more. It is this power of realisation that makes religion; no amount of doctrines or philosophies, or ethical books, that you may have stuffed into your brain, will matter much — only what you *are* and what you have *realised*.

** ** **

To go and say, "Lord, take care of this thing and give me that; Lord, I give you my little prayer and you give me this thing of daily necessity; Lord, cure my headache", and all that — these are not Bhakti. They are the lowest states of religion. They are the lowest form of Karma. If a man uses all his mental energy in seeking to satisfy his body and its wants, show me that difference between him and an animal. Bhakti is a higher thing, higher than even desiring heaven. The idea of heaven is of a place of intensified enjoyment. How can that be God?

Only the fools rush after sense-enjoyments. It is easy to live in the senses. It is easier to run in the old groove, eating and drinking; but what these modern philosophers want to fell you is to take these comfortable ideas and put the stamp of religion on them. Such a doctrine is dangerous. Death lies in the senses. Life on the plane of the Spirit is the only life, life on any other plane is mere death; the whole of this life can be only described as a gymnasium. We must go beyond it to enjoy real life.

— Swami Vivekananda : *op. cit.,* Vol. V, pp. 265-267.

That spiritual knowledge is the highest of all knowledge and that to attain that knowledge is to cast aside all forms of superstition, unfolds a newer vision of Vivekananda's spiritual philosophy. He hates fanaticism in the name of religion because it is devoid of devotion to spiritual excellence. He denounces comparison between one religion and the other because it is simply nonsensical to differentiate; what is really of importance is *sadhana*, through service towards humanity. That is Bhakti. That is spiritualism. As Vivekananda elucidates,

> As long as *touch-me-not-ism* is your creed and the kitchen-pot your deity, you cannot rise spiritually. All the petty differences between religion and religion are mere word-struggles, nonsense. Everyone thinks, "This is my original idea", and wants to have things his own way. That is how struggles come.
>
> In criticising another, we always foolishly take one especially brilliant point as the whole of our life and compare that with the dark ones in the life of another. Thus we make mistakes in judging individuals.
>
> Through fanaticism and bigotry a religion can be propagated very quickly, but the preaching of that religion is firm-based on solid ground, which gives everyone liberty to his opinions and thus uplifts him to a higher path, though this process is slow.
>
> First deluge the land (India) with spiritual ideas, then other ideas will follow. The gift of spirituality and spiritual knowledge is the highest, for it saves from many and many a birth; the next gift is secular knowledge, as it opens the eyes of human beings towards that spiritual knowledge; the next is the saving of life; and the fourth is the gift of food. * * *
>
> A time comes when one understands that to serve a man even by preparing a *Chhilam* (earthen pipe) of tobacco is far greater than millions of meditations. He who can properly prepare a Chhilam of tobacco can also properly meditate.
>
> —*Ibid.*, pp. 267-268.

Looking upon God as a great spiritual force within, Vivekananda makes a radical approach to religion that embraces Truth as the ultimate symbol of God. It is Truth that endears reality and averts abstraction. It is Truth, again, that makes a new avenue of spiritual emancipation by bringing about a cohesion between morality and immorality, good and evil, virtue and vice. As he directs on the destiny of man in terms of God and religion,

> God is not a king sitting away in one corner of the universe to

> deal out punishment or rewards according to a man's deeds here on earth, and the time when man will know the truth, and stand up and say, 'I am God', am life of His life. Why teach that God is far away when our real nature, our immortal principle is God?
>
> Be not deluded by your religion teaching original sin, for the same religion teaches original purity. When Adam fell, he fell from purity. Purity is our real nature, and to regain that is the object of all religion. All men are pure; all men are good. Some objections can be raised to them, and you ask why some men are brutes? That man you call a brute is like the diamond in the dirt and dust — brush the dust off and it is a diamond, just as pure as if the dust had never been on it, and we must admit that every soul is a big diamond.
>
> — Swami Vivekananda : *op. cit.,* Vol. VII, p. 420.

With such a synchronization of good and evil, pure and impure, Vivekananda advances the spirit of religion as love that is based on the unending force of dynamism. As such, the true spirit of religion negates all differences, because these differences are to be considered as an approach only and never in realty. As a spiritual visionary, he significantly suggests,

> Religion is not the outcome of the weakness of human nature; religion is not here because we fear a tyrant; religion is love, unfolding, expanding, growing. Take the watch — within the little case is machinery and a spring. The spring, when wound up, tries to regain its natural state. You are like the spring in the watch, and it is not necessary that all watches have the same kind of a spring, and it is not necessary that we all have the same religion. And why should we quarrel? If we all had the same ideas the world would be dead. External motion we call action; internal motion is human thought. The stone falls to the earth. You say that it is caused by the law of gravitation. The horse draws the cart and God draws the horse. That is the law of motion. Whirlpools show the strength of the current; stop the current and stagnation ensues. Motion is life. We must have unity and variety. The rose would smell as sweet by any other name, and it does not matter what your religion is called.
>
> —*Ibid.,* pp. 421-422.

It is interesting to note in this connection how Gandhi comes closer to Vivekananda in the concept of God and religion from the standpoint of spiritualism. While explaining the nature and extent of worshipping God, he unfolds the spirit of Bhakti as an 'inward communion' that teaches one the 'language of the heart'. And when religion responds perfectly to the language of the heart true spiritualism paves its avenues in the inward worth of mankind. As he enlightens,

> Prayer is a confession of one's unworthiness and weakness. God has a thousand names or rather, He is Nameless. We may worship or pray to Him by whichever name that pleases us. Some call Him Rama, some Krishna, others call Him Rahim, and yet others call Him God. All worship the same spirit, but as all foods do not agree with all, all names do not appeal to all. Each chooses the name according to his associations, and He being the In-Dweller, All-Powerful and Omniscient knows our innermost feelings and responds to us according to our deserts.
>
> Worship or prayer, therefore, is not to be performed with the lips, but with the heart. And that is why it can be performed equally by the dumb and the stammerer, by the ignorant and the stupid. And the prayer of those whose tongues are nectared but whose hearts are full of poison are never heard. He, therefore, who would pray to God, must cleanse his heart. * * * It is faith that steers us through stormy seas; faith that moves mountains and faith that jumps across the ocean. That faith is nothing but a living, wide awake consciousness of God within. He who has achieved that faith wants nothing. Bodily diseased he is spiritually healthy, physically pure, he rolls in spiritual riches.
>
> — M.K. Gandhi : *Young India*, September 24, 1925.

Elucidating further the way to learn the 'language of the heart' from a Bhakta, Gandhi exposes the spiritual vision of God in service towards mankind, specially towards the supposed ones :

> The language of the lips is easily taught but who can reach the language of the heart? Only the Bhakta — the true devotee — knows it and can teach it. The Gita has defined the Bhakta in three places, and talked of him generally everywhere. But a

knowledge of the definition of a Bhakta is hardly a sufficient guide. They are rare on this earth. I have, therefore, suggested the Religion of Service as the means. God of Himself seeks for His seat the heart of him who serves his fellowmen. * * *

But who are the suffering and the woe-begone? The suppressed and the poverty-stricken. He who would be a Bhakta, therefore, must serve these by body, soul and mind. How can he who regards the "suppressed" classes as untouchables serve them by the body? He who does not even condescend to exert his body to the extent of spinning for the sake of the poor and trots out lame excuses does not know the meaning of service. An able-bodied wretch deserves nc alms, but an appeal to work for his bread. Alms debase him. He who spins before the poor inviting them to do likewise serves God as no one else does. "He who gives me even a trifle as a fruit or a flower or even a leaf in the spirit of Bhakti is my servant", says the Lord in the Bhagvadgita. As he hath his foot-stool where live "The humble, the lowliest and lost", spinning therefore, for such is the greatest prayer, the greatest worship, the greatest sacrifice.

—*Ibid.*

The symbolic interpretation of God as a great spiritual force in the form of service towards mankind finds a similar echo in Vivekananda who values work as the primary component of spiritual emancipation of humanity. His God is both work and worship in manifold dimensions. While explaining true religion, he unfolds the spiritual and aesthetic dimensions of human endeavour in achieving slowly but certainly the desired goal of perfection as a divine Being. Admittedly, he shows the dynamic role of every human being by means of adherence to and observance of practical spiritualism. As he characteristically spells out,

True religion comes not from the teaching of men or the reading of books; it is the awakening of the spirit within us, consequent upon pure and heroic action. Every child born into the world brings with it a certain accumulated experience from previous incarnations; and the impress of this experience is seen in the structure of its mind and body. But the feeling of independence which possesses us all shows there is something in us besides mind and body. The soul that reigns within is independent and creates the desire for freedom. If we are not free, how can we hope to make the world better? We hold that human progress is the result of the action of the human spirit. What the world is, and what we ourselves are, are the fruits of the freedom of the spirit.

We believe in one God, the Father of us all, who is omnipresent and omnipotent, and who guides and preserves His children with infinite love. We believe in a Personal God as the Christians do, but we go further : we believe that we are He! That His personality is manifested in us, that God is in us, and that we are in God. We believe there is a germ of truth in all religion, and the Hindu bows down to them all; for in this world, truth is to be found not in subtraction but in addition. We would offer God a bouquet of the most beautiful flowers of all the diverse faiths. We must love God for love's sake, not for the hope of reward. We must do our duty for duty's sake, not for the hope of reward. We must worship the beautiful for beauty's sake, not for the hope of reward. Thus in the purity of our hearts shall we see God. Sacrifices, genuflexions, mumblings, and mutterings are not religion. They are only good if they stimulate us to the brave performance of beautiful and heroic deeds and lift our thoughts to the apprehension of the divine perfection.

What good is it, if we acknowledge in our prayers that God is the Father of us all, and in our daily lives do not treat every man as our brother? Books are only made so that they may point the way to a higher life; but no good results unless the path is trodden with unflinching steps. Every human personality may be compared to a glass globe. There is the same pure white light — an emission of the divine Being — in the centre of each, but the glass being of different colours and thickness, the rays assume diverse aspects in the transmission. The equality and beauty of each central flame is the same, and the apparent inequality is only in the imperfection of the temporal instrument of its expression. As we rise higher and higher in the scale of being, the medium becomes more and more translucent.

— Swami Vivekananda : *op. cit.*, Vol IV, pp. 190-191.

In the pursuit of excellence, man's endeavour as elucidated above comes rather as a force from within than from without just as a swan's own endeavour to have the pure milk out of water. But, then, the spiritual vision of the All Serene in case of every human being is an endless journey of beyonding from being[2] as Vivekananda rightly suggests in scaling the steps of perfection higher and higher. Viewing religion as an experience, and Love as God, Vivekananda emphasizes on being and becoming as the end in view of religion. As a spiritual optimist like Gandhi he holds the spirit of man higher than any earthly possession. In fact, he urges on the beyonding of each 'I' to be in unison with the All Beautiful in realization and perfection. His clarion call as a spiritual emancipator of mankind bears evidence as follows:

> Never say man is weak. Wisdom-Yoga is no better than the others. Love is the ideal and requires no object. Love is God. So even through devotion we reach the subjective God. I am He How can one work, unless one loves city, country, animals, the universe? Reason leads to the finding of unity in variety. Let the atheist and the agnostic work for the social good. So God comes.
>
> But this you must guard against : Do not disturb the faith of any. For you must know that religion is not in doctrines. Religion lies in being and becoming, in realisation. All men are born idolaters. The lowest man is an animal. The highest man is perfect. And between these two, all have to think in sound and colour, in doctrine and ritual.
>
> The test of having ceased to be an idolater is: "When you say 'I', does the body come into your thought or not? If it does then you are still a worshipper of idols". Religion is not intellectual jargon at all, but realization, If you *think* about God, you are only a fool. The ignorant man, by prayer and devotion, can reach beyond the philosopher. To know God, no philosophy is necessary. Our duty is not to disturb the faith of others. Religion is experience. above all and in all, be sincere; identification brings misery, because it brings desire. Thus the poor man sees gold, and identifies himself with the need of gold. Be the witness. *Learn never to react.*
>
> *Ibid.*

Gandhi makes the path of self-realization more assured when he gives importance to *brahmacharya* as a means of spiritual introspection. This is the way to be in the true spirit of self-endurance for self-realization besides which religion and for that matter the beyonding of being becomes an abstraction. In fact, the radical change of the world after the Second World War has brought forth the spiritual vision of his principles of truth and non-violence as a more important component of the inner worth of man than anything else. As he significantly observes,

> There has been cataclysmic changes in the world. Do I adhere still to my faith in truth and non-violence? Has not the atom bomb exploded that faith? Not only has it done so, but it has clearly demonstrated to me that the twins constitute the mightiest force in the world. Before it the atom bomb is of no effect. The two opposing forces are wholly different in kind, the one moral and spiritual, the other physical and material. The one is infinitely superior to the other which by its very nature has an end. The force of spirit is ever progressive and endless. Its full expression makes it unconquerable in the world. In saying so I know that I have said nothing new. I merely bear witness to the fact. What is more, that force resides in everybody, man, woman and child, irrespective of the colour of the skin. Only, in many, it lies dormant, but it is capable of being awakened by judicious training.
>
> — D.G. Tendulkar : *Mahatma, op. cit.,* Vol. VII, p. 53.

For a 'judicious training' in spiritualism, while Vivekananda emphasizes on *Bhakti-Yoga* and *Jnana-Yoga,* Gandhi deserves everyone to follow the principles of a true *Vaishnava* to be inspired with the ideal of spiritual sanctity. The *pad* by the Gujarati poet Narsi Mehta, which is a living inspiration and one of his most beloved hymns speaks how one should aim at spiritual emancipation to be in unison with the All Serene :

Vaishnava jana to tene Kahiye
Call that one a true *Vaishnava*
        Who feels the suffering of others,
Who seeks to relieve others' pain
        and has no pride in his soul (Refrain)

He bows respectfully to the whole world,
        he talks ill of no one;
He remains steadfast in mind, worlds and action :

blessed, blessed be his mother
He is impartial to all, he has renounced all greed,
he sees another man's wife as his own mother,
His tongue speaks no lie,
he does not touch another man's property.

He remains unaffected by *maya* and *moha*,
in his soul is total detachment;
He remains absorbed in meditation on Ram's Name,
within his body, all the *tirthas* are found.

Without cupidity or guile is he,
without lust or anger
Says Narsaiyo, by the mere view of such a Sant,
seventy-two generations find salvation.

— '*Gujarati Bhajan*', *Ashram-bhajanavali*, Prakashan Press, Ahmedabad, No. 102, p. 135. Translated by Charlotte Vaudeville, Quoted from "*Sant Mat* : Santism as the Universal Path to Sanctity", *The Sants* Ed. by Karine Schomer & W.H. Mc. Leod, Berkeley Religious Studies Series, Motilal Banarsidass, New Delhi, 1987, pp. 39-40.

Being deeply inspired with the immortal sayings of the *Gita*, Vivekananda also humbly prays for emancipation from all forms of *Maya*. In one of his letters, he quotes the following lines of the *Gita* and observes,

Apuryamanamachalapratishthang
Samudramapah pravisanti yadvat
Tadvat kama yang pravisanti sarve
Sa santimapnoti na kamakami

("Not he that lusteth after objects of desire, but he alone obtaineth peace in whom desires lose themselves like river-water flowing into the ocean but leaving it unaffected and unmodified in spite of constant accession".)

— *The Gita*, II, 70.

> Bless me that my heart may wax strong with supreme strength Divine, and that all forms of Maya may drop off from me for aye : "We have taken up the Cross, Thou hast laid it upon us and grant us strength that we bear it unto death. Amen". *Imitation of Christ.*
>
> — Swami Vivekananda : "Epistles", *op. cit.*, Vol. VI, p. 207.

For a totality of being which equates one to spiritual excellence, Gandhi also advocates for illumination of the divine strength in oneself and to eliminate the difference between heaven and earth. The earth to be a true earth for mankind must be a heaven to sing the glory of the All Glorious. Therefore, as a spiritual apostle singing the saga of spiritual action throughout his life in devotion and dedication, he wants to hold the Kingdom of heaven on earth 'to see God face to face' in the mirror of human action. Rejecting the usual concept of the world as it is, he observes in connection with the practice of non-violence :

> To practise non-violence in mundane matters is to know its true value. It is to bring heaven upon earth. There is no such thing as the other world. All worlds are one. There is no 'here' and no 'there'. As Jeans has demonstrated, the whole universe including the most distant stars, invisible even through the most powerful telescope in the world, is compressed in an atom. I hold it therefore to be wrong to limit the use of non-violence to cave-dwellers and for acquiring merit for a favoured position in the other world. All virtue ceases to have use if it serves no purpose in every walk of life.
>
> — M.K. Gandhi : *Harijan*, July 26, 1942.

Vivekananda, of course, evaluates the world in terms of good and evil with which one is associated, by conceiving it at the outset as a 'gymnasium', for perfection of humanity. He advocates for spiritually visualizing both the good and the evil in beyonding so that one might be enkindled with spiritual magnificence. As he poignantly observes,

> This universe of ours, the universe of the senses, the rational, the intellectual, is bounded on both sides by the illimitable, the unknowable, the ever unknown. Herein is the search, herein are

the inquiries, here are the facts; from this comes the light which is known to the world as religion. Essentially, however, religion belongs to the supersensuous and not to the sense plane. It is beyond all reasoning, and not on the plane of intellect. It is a vision, an inspiration, a plunge into the unknown and unknowable, making the unknowable more than known for it can never be "known". This search has been in the human mind, as I believe, from the very beginning of humanity. There cannot have been human reasoning and intellect in any period of the world's history without this struggle, this search beyond. In our little universe, this human mind, we see a thought arise. Whence it rises we do not know, and when it disappears, where it goes, we know not either. The macrocosm and the microcosm are, as it were, in the same groove, passing through the same stages, vibrating in the same key.

** ** **

This world is neither good nor evil. It is the Lord's World. It is beyond both good and evil, perfect in itself. His will is going on, showing all these different pictures; and it will go on without beginning and without end. It is a great gymnasium in which you and I, and millions of souls must come and get exercises, and make ourselves strong and perfect. This is what it is for. Not that God could not make a perfect universe; not that He could not help the misery of the world.

— Swami Vivekananda : "The Claims of Religion", *op. cit.*, Vol. IV, pp. 203-207.

Realizing that the spiritual endeavour of mankind should be geared to the practical purpose of perfection to be attained through purity of action, Gandhi also considers spirituality in terms of direct experiences of one single Brotherhood of Mankind. None is spiritual in the sense that none is devoted to the discovery of one's own being in relation to others residing far or near and, at the same time, to that of one's beyonding. This is the exercise of true spiritualism, true consciousness of *Ekatvatva* — oneness. To believe and act according to this concept of spiritualism is to feel and acknowledge the All Beautiful in every living being, thereby acknowledging the spiritual vision of

Swami Vivekananda — *Yatra jeev tatra Shiv* — where there are living beings there is the All Serene. So one cannot but practically approach towards the well-being of the entire humanity for the cause of one's spiritual enlightenment. Gandhi also categorically asserts,

> If any action of mine claimed to be spiritual is proved to be unpractical it must be pronounced to be a failure. I do believe that the most spiritual act is the most practical in the true sense of the term.
>
> — M.K. Gandhi : *Harijan*, July 1, 1939.

Whatever action Gandhi contemplates and introduces is, therefore, a synchronization of 'moral effort and spiritual experience' for true exposition of religion. This is actually the dynamics of religion in spiritual action as highlighted by Swami Vivekananda in the remaking and re-shaping of religion to negotiate all ills of the world. The Gandhian pattern of spiritualism, indeed, makes a harmonious blending of faith, conduct and knowledge in continual efflorescence of consciousness.[3] This is how Gandhi wants 'to see God face to face'. As R.R. Diwakar obseves,

> Gandhi's personal aspiration and ambition was, as he himself has stated in his own words, 'to see God face to face'. There is no greater or more ambitious aspirations to be found professed by any mystic or saint in the whole hagiology of the world. God here is obviously a synonym for the Supreme Spiritual Power or Gnostic Energy pervading and immanent in all existence past, present and future. From time immemorial spiritual and religious saints and sages have laid down and practised disciplines for achieving this spiritual goal, namely seeing 'God face to face' or what is commonly described as 'Self-realization' or 'God-realization', 'Atmajnan' or 'Atmanubhuti', the realization that, what we call 'I', the 'Atman', is not the body or life of mind or all these put together, but a spiritual entity which is one with some tangible power or Energy which transcends the realm of cognisible world and yet exists in an eternal, infinite Existence behind and beyond all phenomena we normally experience. Firmly rooted in this faith, Gandhi struck an unorthodox path to achieve and attain an orthodox goal, and that path was the selfless, tireless service of

the poorest, the lowest and the hardest-hit human beings as well as all sentient creatures.

— R.R. Diwakar : *Gandhi, the Spiritual Seeker,* Bharatiya Vidya Bhavan, Bombay, p. 778.

To feel oneness of all and to extend that feeling in the form of transcendence is the core of Gandhian spiritualism. It echoes the very pattern of feeling of the All Beautiful in diverse action for service towards the entire humanity as time and again pronounced and proved in poignance of action by Swami Vivekananda. It fully admits the latter's spiritual vision of the object of *Bhakti* that is unison with God by a refinement of love. Such a pattern of love allows everyone to rise beyond personal love and extend the finer sensibilities of love to be in cohesion with the Absolute. In Vivekananda's words,

> Bhakti or worship or love in some form or other is the easiest, pleasantest, and most natural way of man. The natural state of this universe is attraction and that is surely followed by an ultimate disunion. Even so, love is the natural impetus of union in the human heart; and though itself a great cause of misery, properly directed towards the proper object, it brings deliverance. The object of Bhakti is God. Love cannot be without a subject and an object. The object of love again must be at first a being who can reciprocate our love. Therefore the God of love must be in some sense a human God. He must be God of love. Aside from the question whether such a God exists or not, it is a fact that to those who have love in their heart this Absolute appears as God of love, as personal.
>
> The lower forms of worship, which embody the idea of God as a judge or punisher or someone to be obeyed through fear, do not deserve to be called love, although they are forms of worship gradually expanding into higher forms. We pass on to the consideration of love itself. We will illustrate love by a triangle, of which the first angle at the base is fearlessness. So long as there is fear, it is not love. Love banishes all fear. A mother with her baby will face a tiger to save her child. The second angle is that love never asks, never begs. The third of the apex is that love loves for the sake of love itself. Even the ideas of object vanishes. Love is the only form in which love is loved. This is the highest abstrac-

tion and the same as the Absolute.

—Swami Vivekananda : 'Four Paths of Yoga', *op. cit.*, Vol. VIII, pp. 153-154.

Considering human life as an inseparable part of all-round fulness, Gandhi, like Vivekananda, also gives importance to a harmonious ascent of man from ordinary to spiritual height in course a daily activities. As he remarks,

> Human life, being an undivided whole, on line could be drawn between ethics and politics. A trader who earned his wealth by deception only succeeded in deceiving himself when he thought that his sins could be washed away by spending some amount of his ill-gotten gains on so-called religious purposes. One's everyday life was never capable of being separated from his spiritual being.

M.K. Gandhi : *Harijan,* March 30, 1947.

The spiritual concept of Love as Vivekananda and Gandhi highlight may be expressed in the following tabular forms :

Table : A

The Triangle of Love : The Spiritual Dimensions

Love for Love
or
Absolute Love

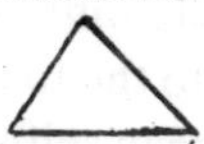

Fearlessness Love *sans* return
sans self

Table : B

The Orbit of Love : The Spiritual Dimensions

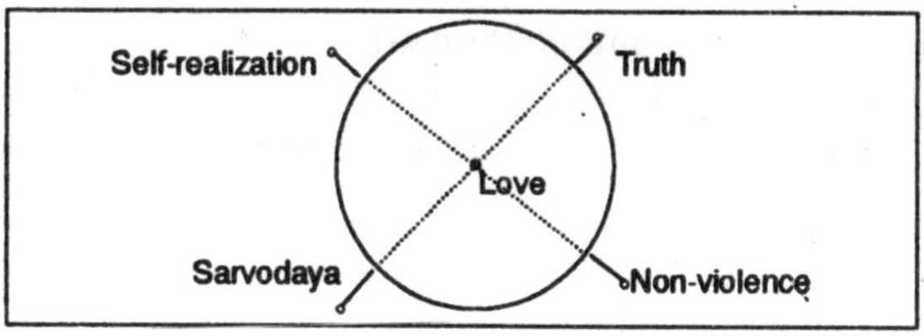

From the above two tables 'A' and 'B' representing the spiritual dimensions of love as elucidated by Vivekananda and Gandhi, it is evident that the centre of interest for poignance of spiritualism is the gradual ascent of man for fusion with the All Serene. The being must transcend for the beyonding in order to have the true spiritual vision of the All Serene. This is why Gandhi believes in Spirituality in action:

> For Gandhi, God had no 'form' nor was God a Person. In other words, he believed in a Spiritual Presence everywhere and all the time behind and beyond all phenomenal existence — that presence alone was the Eternal Reality. For Gandhi, God was Truth, God was Love, God was Law, God was Life and God was everything that existed in the past, that exists in the present, and that will ever exist in the future.
>
> — R.R. Diwakar : "Gandhi is Spirituality in Action", *Gandhi Marg*, Journal of the Gandhi Peace Foundation, New Delhi, Vol. VI, No. 11, February 1985. pp. 773-774.

Simultaneously, let us christen ourselves with the spiritual vision of Love of Swami Vivekananda :

Let go your vain reliance on knowledge,
Let go your prayers, offerings and strength,
For Love selfless is the only resource; -
Lo, the insects teach, embracing the flame;
The basis insect's blind, by beauty charmed,
Thy soul is drunken with the wine of Love;
O thou Lover true, cast into the fire
All thy drops of self, thy mean selfishness.

Say — comes happiness e'er to a beggar?
What good being object of charity?
Give away, ne'er turn to ask in return,
Should there be the wealth treasured in thy heart.

Ay, born heir to the Infinite thou art,
Within the heart is the ocean of Love,
"Give", "Give away" — whoever asks return,

His ocean dwindles down to a mere drop.
From highest Brahman to the younder worm,
And to the very minutest atom,
Everywhere is the same God, the All-Love
Friend, offer mind, soul, body, at their feet.

These are His manifold forms before thee,
Rejecting them, where seekers thou for God?
Who loves all beings without distinction,
He indeed is worshipping best his God.

— Swami Vivekananda : "To a Friend", *op. cit.,* Vol. IV, pp. 495-496

NOTES

1. In a letter to an American friend, Romain Rolland delineates his impressions about Gandhi, which give an insight into the cohesion of spiritual consciousness between Gandhi and Vivekananda :

His [*Gandhi's*] mind proceeds through successive experiments into action, and he follows a straight line, but he never stops, and one would risk an error in attempting to judge him by what he said ten years ago because his thought is in constant revolution. I will give you now a little example of it that is characteristic.

He was asked at Lausanne to define what he understood by God. He explained how, among the noblest attributes which the Hindu scriptures ascribed to God, he had in his youth chosen the word 'truth' as most truly defining the essential element. He had said, 'God is Truth'. But he added, 'two years ago I advanced another step. I now say, 'Truth is God'. For, even the atheists do not doubt the necessity for the power of truth. In their passion for discovering the truth, the atheists have not hesitated to deny the existence of God, and, from their point of view, they are right. You will understand from this single trait the boldness and independence of this religious spirit from the Orient. I noted in him traits similar to Vivekananda.

— Quoted from D.G. Tendulkar : *Mahatma*, Publications Division, Ministry of Information and Broadcasting, Government of India, Vol. III, pp. 149-150.

2. Sri Aurobindo also emphasizes on the same necessity of spiritual transformation. The 'right road to become ourselves' is to be dynamic to this extent of the beyonding of being endlessly. As he observes,

We see that at first man seems to be a double nature, animal and rational. All his unease comes from man's practical failure to solve the riddle and difficulty of his double nature. The higher life of reason is still something that is superimposed on the lower. It is so even with rare individuals, there is a dominance, but not a transformation. Life cannot be entirely rational, mind is not the destined archangel of the transformation. As a reaction against such chimercial ideals the mind is then used — as seems to be the case with modern civilisation — as a slave of life and body. The result has been a vital titanism, and it has ended badly, as it always must. For a while the pressure of events has forced a nobler ethics and reason as a means for the better ordering of individual, national and international life.. But this, well-enough for a first step, is not the real and final solution.

For that we have to return to the pursuit of an ancient secret, the ideal of the Kingdom of God. This cannot be done, as past attempts show, either by a divorce between life and spirit or a departure into other worlds or a compromise or by a superimposing of the spiritual life or some of its ideas and motives on the mental, vital and physical life. This is the most that human society has done in the past.

The secret of the transformation lies in the transference of our centre of living to a higher consciousness and in a change of our main power of being. All that we have done so far is some half successful effort to transfer will and power to the mental plane. To complete this upward transference we must go further, choose between the domination of the vital part in us and the spontaneous obedience of the spiritualised man to the truth of his own realised being, which will be other and greater than the limited perfection of arrested development we see already accomplished in the working of physical Nature. Hence this perfection cannot come by the mental idea dealing with the Spirit — that was Asia's mistake — as it deals with life. For the mind and the intellect are not the key powers of our existence. Only when this transference and the dynamic transformation that follows it have been completed we shall be on the right road to become ourselves, live in our true, satisfied self-existence in our real being and divine nature.

— Sri Aurobindo : *The Human Cycle*, Abridged and Edited by Sisirkumar Ghose, Sri Aurobindo Pathamandir, Calcutta, 1972, pp. 79-80

3. With Gandhiji, religion was no formal profession, it was a moral effort and spiritual experience embracing faith and conduct, action, feeding knowledge and knowledge illuminating action.

— 'Preface', *The Collected Works of Mahatma Gandhi*, Publications Division, Ministry of Information and Broadcasting, Government of India, April 1969, Vol. XXXII, p. viii.

8

GANDHIAN SPIRITUALISM AND THE MODERN WORLD

> This little man has been and is a colossus before whom others, big in their own way and in their own space and time, are small of stature. In this world of hatred and uttermost violence and the atom bomb, this man of peace and good-will stands out, a contrast and a challenge. In an acquisitive society madly searching for new gadgets and new luxuries, he takes to his loincloth and his mud hut. In man's race for wealth and authority and power, he seems to be a non-starter, looking the other way; and yet that authority looks out of his gentle but hard eyes, that power seems to fill his slight and ematiated frame, and flows out to others. Wherein does his strength lie, wherein this power and authority? Has he drunk somewhere from the secret spring of life which has given strength to India through the ages?
>
> – Jawaharlal Nehru: 'Foreword', *Mahatma Gandhi*, Asia Publishing House, Bombay 1949, p. 7.

The discovery of the 'little man' in endless queries as above remains flooded in wonders of wonders. The 'little man' remains great or perhaps above greatness, for he *is* even when he is not within ourselves as a mortal being. The living message of spiritualism as he has left behind beckons the modern world with the brightest hope of regeneration of humanism. A modern world booed and barricaded in the desert of futility and desolation springs again with the elimination of the self and embrace of all for the All Beautiful. Here, then, is this 'little man' who proclaims to the modern world for the first time in the history of man to be little about oneself in order to be great and enjoy the effulgence of greatness in the greatness of others.

Why is Gandhian spiritualism still to be pondered over and

honoured for a reshaping of the modern world? What are the essential contributing factors of his spiritual vision that highlight India as the foremost propagator of spiritual excellence in the world? Why are his strategies for bringing out all-round goodness in humanity necessitate a rethinking in terms of the modern ukase in spiritualism? "My life is my message", so says Gandhi about himself, as everyone knows. And moreover, with the self-education received by means of an intensive study of the Indian mystic and spiritual traditions, he prepares himself for spiritual dedication to the welfare of global humanity.[1] Enriched with an orphic voice that translates spiritualism from the most practical aspects and visions of life, Gandhi remains an ever-abiding spirit of modernism. As Loui's Renou characteristically sums up,

> . . . Gandhi successfully reflected the latent aspirations of a people. It is not in Moslem or Pre-Moslem history that we must look first for his examples. Ancient India did not lack enlightened princes or great spiritual leaders, beginning with the extraordinary figure of the Buddha. But the former (almost without exception) laid no claim to act in the name of a moral order: when they withdrew from the world, at least according to tradition, they did so for their personal salvation, they entered the path of 'deliverance'. And the later ones, though men of action in their own way, like Sankara or Ramanuja, who directed religious propaganda, never pretended to play a religious role. The Buddha resolutely set himself above temporal values, accepting the Brahminic Society of his day and keeping to the forms of the Hindu dharma. There is only one exception: the Emperor Asoka in the third century before our era. He became the master of almost the whole of India after a series of bloody wars and conquests, then suddenly abandoned this policy and inaugurated a reign of justice and merely based on dharma. But a man who seizes power, and, after attaining his ends, renounces the means to which he owes success, is one thing; the man who starts from nothing and reaches the highest rank by the most unpromising methods is another.
>
> On the whole, we must look for Gandhi's fore-runners in the leaders of sects, the countless men who 'cleared paths' and 'opened up ways'. In the middle ages and up to the present, there are examples of such men, coming from all social and spiritual

> strata, gathering communities about them, adopting new gospels, sometimes trying to make their way in the social or political field by means which they invariably claimed to derive from those gospels. Such are Basava in the 12th century with the Lingayats: Ramananda and Kabir in the 15th century, Nanak, the founder of the Sikhs, in the 15th and 16th centuries. But what these men viewed in terms of the locality and of the needs of the sect, Gandhi conceived for India as a whole.
>
> – Louis Renou: "Gandhi and Indian Civilization", *The Visva-Bharati Quarterly*, Gandhi Number, Visva-Bharati, Santiniketan, Vol. 35, pp. 51-52.

The vision of a world spiritualized in the beyonding of consciousness as Gandhi always propagates is the poetry yet written in terms of all-round excellence of humanism. From intimation of the eternal within in course of pursuit of Truth to inward contemplation of the presence of God for the joyous communion of the soul with God that extends towards march of the alone to the Alone is the thrilling adventure yet to be made. Gandhi calls for an ardent preparation to march onward for the fulfilment of that prayer through spiritual endeavour of humanity. To act as an humble servant for global spiritual enrichment is to be forechristened with how and why Gandhi sticks to truth and goodness under varying circumstances. Indeed, the death he encounters in course of his prayer is glorified in the spiritual ecstasy.[2]

The dawn of a new era of spiritual effulgence in the modern world awaits a ripening of values that we cherish spiritually. The good old days of humanity are an antidote to erosion of values and sense and sensibilities we come across off and on in the global society. Hearts today are torn apart in scissored ambitions in utilitarianism – the wailing of the doomed hearts of modernity. A revival of the brotherhood of man by means of spiritual awakening in strengthening the inner spirit of man both nationally and internationally as shown by Gandhi in his simplicity of action and truth, devotion and endearment is the only way to avert global incoherence. As Carlos Romulo observes,

> The idea of the brotherhood of men is of course an ancient precept. Perhaps it was Gandhi who first, and to such an extent, waged a political struggle based on the idea and, logically,

> rejected those means, no doubt open to him, which would violate the principle of non-injury. This is also what makes for Gandhi's continuing relevance: the fact that he conceived of a type of politics, not based on the advantage of a nation, nor on the superiority of arms, nor yet on the basis of class struggle. This is the uniqueness of Gandhi's politics and this is ultimately what the world must come to terms with.
>
> Gandhi gave the idea of the brotherhood of men its significant definition at a time when nationalism had something to do with the setting of limits on national boundaries; with the insane division of peoples into the confines of geographical or cultural domains; and with the setting up of barricades, as it were, in terms of military strength to conserve the very artificial apartness of peoples. He opposed British rule on the concept of unity.
>
> I would think that the world today has no other choice but to move towards the very simplicity and directness and truth of Gandhi's principle. The resurgence of will in the international community, expressed by the awakening of people previously subjugated, by citizens traditionally coerced by the so-called rule of law, and by the youth all over the world, has but one message to the contemporary consciousness; that solidarity could yet be presented by men, with no means to enforce their will but the moral force of their number and status in society, against the policies of governments that tend to divide, rather than integrate, the family of man.
>
> – Carlos Romulo: "Truth and Nonviolence in Gandhi's Humanism", *Truth and Nonviolence*, Edited by T.K. Mahadevan, Gandhi Peace Foundation, New Delhi, 1970, pp. 323-324.

That politics cannot efface the consciousness of humanity is the core of Gandhian spiritualism which runs in an introspective pattern of sincere endeavour towards emancipation of man. This indeed, is realization of the All Beautiful from the supreme spiritual end in view for which be becomes a martyr to fullness of vision. The cathedral of inner consciousness that Gandhi wants to uphold in a World Spiritual is the cathedral of finding joy in the Eternal by means of achieving joy in the glory of global humanity. It is the action of all actions ably guided by spiritual devotion. It is the action of all actions that pulsate humanity to transcend from being to beyonding.

It is the action of all actions that virtually makes man a partner to the All Beautiful in total effulgence of Light. As a spiritual apostle of human excellence, Gandhi, like himself, wants the world humanity to be on the serene avenue of spiritual endeavour as it is elucidated in the *Upanishad*:

> *Ishavasyamidang sarva yatking cha jagatyang jagat*
> *Tena tyaktena bhujithah ma gridhah kasyachiddhanam.*
> *Hiranmayena patrena satyashyapihitang mukham*
> *Tattvang pushan apavrinu satyadharmaya dristaye.*
>
> *Isha Upanishad*. 1.15

> Behold the Universe in the glory of
> God; and all that lives and moves on earth.
> Leaving the transient, find joy in the
> Eternal: set not your heart on another's possession.
> The face of truth remains hidden
> behind a circle of gold
> Unveil it, O God of light, that
> I who love the true may see
>
> *Isha Upanishad*, Verses 1 & 15

– Translated by J. Mascare, Quoted from *In Search of the Supreme* by M.K. Gandhi, Navajivan Publishing House, Ahmedabad, 1961, p. viii.

To behold the face of truth in the light of spiritual consciousness is as Gandhi strongly advocates, to behold the inner man within every man. It is what one normally fails to identify in one's self-confidence, and, as a consequence, cannot utilize it as a shield of God. Conversely, when one cultivates self-confidence and makes God one's shield the world becomes one's very own. Then the numerous little forms of differences and incoherences are brushed aside by means of a fusion of spiritual vastness in self-purification. As Gandhi foresees in spiritual vision,

> We are today weighed down by our own selfishness and parochialism of outlook, we must cast it out. We know how to die for our family but it is time that we learn to go a step further. We must widen the circle of our love till it embraces the whole village,

> the village in its turn must take into fold the district, the district the province, and so on till the scope of our love becomes co-terminous with the world. * * * You must cultivate self-confidence and make God your shield. There is none mightier than He.
>
> – M.K. Gandhi: *Young India*, June 27, 1929.

With such a christening of spiritualism, the global man awaits a revamping of the Spirit Eternal. The dreams of a better world of tomorrow beckons the Gandhian quest for the essence of excellence in education and in religion, in the ethics of *Sarvodaya* or in the Gandhian aesthetics of the True, the Good and the Beautiful. To explore the world as it is in its truant and bizarre modernity is to explore anew in the spirit of human consciousness – undaunted, sombre and challenging in the pursuit of the worth of man as man. And so, whether in the pattern of *ahimsa* or *sarvodaya, charkha* or *nai talim*, the end in view as Gandhi solemnly realizes and translates into reality, is always unison with the All Serene – The Sprit Eternal. Gandhi of course, heightens his course of action and contemplation in the quest for the beyonding of being for he earnestly believes that the spiritual quest in any form whatsoever is the adoration of the Holy Grail – the Light of Lights in mankind.

For a modern world *sans* modernity and happy in triggered toying with conscience, Gandhi is the lone sentinel who makes us alert as Tagore does to listen to the music of the night:

> Misery knocks at thy door, and her message is that thy lord is wakeful and he calls thee to the love-tryst through the darkness of night.
>
> The sky is overcast with clouds and the rain is ceaseless. I know not what this is that stirs in me — I know not its meaning.
>
> A moment's flash of lightning drags down a deeper gloom on my sight, and my heart gropes for the path to where the music of the night calls me.
>
> – Rabindranath Tagore: *Gitanjali (Song Offerings)*, Macmillan India Limited, Macmillan Pocket Tagore Edition, 1983, No. XXVII, p. 16.

Admittedly, the modern world misrepresented in manifold miseries of mankind engulfs the spiritual quest for excellence. But, then, to be a servant of the Great Master is to embrace any eventuality as the Light of lights eternally burns. What Gandhi has uttered on the night of January 29, 1948 bears testimony to this truth:

> If I die of a lingering illness, nay even by as much as a boil or a pimple, it will be your duty to proclaim to the world, even at the risk of making people angry with you, that I was not the man of God that I claimed to be. If you do that it will give my spirit peace. Note down this also that if someone were to end my life by putting a bullet through me – as someone tried to do with a bomb the other day – and I met his bullet without a groan, and breathed my last taking God's name, then alone would I have made good my claim.
>
> – Pyarelal: *Mahatma Gandhi, The Last Phase*, Navajivan Publishing House, Ahmedabad, 1958, Vol. II, p. 766.

What a lesson for the modern world to be in the serene feeling of spiritual denouement!

NOTES

1. While evaluating Gandhi's contribution to the modern world, Professor P.C. Roychoudhury observes,

> Gandhi had inherited the mystic tradition of Indian culture and had appreciated the spiritual significance of it. It is doubtful if he attempted deliberately to invent any new ideas. In a way he rediscovered the significance of the traditional concepts and tried their practical application in everyday life to solve the problems of the world as it is. He was basically a child of the Indian tradition but in his voyage of rediscovering the truth of the Indian concepts he depended largely on Tolstoy, Ruskin and Emerson. He drank deep from the fountains of the authoritative literature of different religions. The Bible, the Quran and the Gita were his source of inspiration. The Sermon on the Mount was as important to him as the Bhajans. Hindu religion was soul-satisfying, as Gandhi used to say. But he made a distinction between true Hinduism and the various superstitions and spurious traditions that had crept into Hinduism. He did not accept that untouchability was a part of the creed of Hinduism. On the other hand, he thought that untouchability was a disgrace. It is his breadth of mind that gave him a sense of identity with men of different religious faiths.
>
> It is difficult to say which was the more important contribution of Gandhi to

the world, his ethical attitude, his contribution to social regeneration or his political work. Once Professor Tucci had observed that as a student of Indian culture he was concerned more with the ethical attitude of Gandhi and according to him Gandhi in his enunciation of truth and non-violence had placed greater emphasis on action than on mere intellectual recognition of their values. Professor Tucci thought that Gandhi wanted to find an answer to the problems of today in ancient values of religion and that the best tribute one could pay to him is to try to live according to his teachings.

— P.C. Roychoudhury: "Gandhi: A Revaluation", *The Visva-Bharati Quarterly*, Gandhi Number, Visva-Bharati, Santiniketan, Vol. 35, Nos. 1-4 (Combined), pp. 44-45.

2. Jawaharlal Nehru makes a very poignant evaluation of Mahatma Gandhi as an incomparable and illustrious spiritual crusader as follows:

We mourn for Bapu and feel orphaned. Looking back at his magnificent life, what is there to mourn for? Surely to very very few human beings in history could it have been given to find so much fulfilment in their own lives. He was sad for our failures and unhappy at not having raised India to greater heights. That sadness and unhappiness are easy to understand. Yet who dares say that his life was a failure? Whatever he touched he turned into something worthwhile and precious. Whatever he did yielded substantial results, though perhaps not as great as he hoped for. One carried away the impression that he could not really fail in anything that he attempted. According to the teachings of the Gita, he laboured dispassionately without attachment to results and so results came to him.

During his long life, full of hard work and activity and novel adventures out of the common rut, there is hardly any jarring note anywhere. All his manifold activities became progressively a symphony and every word he spoke and every gesture that he made fitted into this, and so unconsciously he became the perfect artist, for he had learned the art of living, though the way of life he had adopted was very different from the worlds way. It became apparent that the pursuit of truth and goodness leads among other things to this artistry in life.

As he grew older his body seemed to be just a vehicle for the mighty spirit within him. Almost one forgot the body as one listened to him or looked at him, and so where he sat became a temple and where he trod was a hallowed ground.

Even in his death there was a magnificence and complete artistry. It was from every point of view a fitting climax to the man and to the life he had lived. Indeed it heightened the lesson of his life. He died in the fullness of his powers and as he would no doubt have liked to die, at the moment of prayer.

— Jawaharlal Nehru: *Mahatma Gandhi*, Asia Publishing House, Bombay, 1949, pp. 158-159.

9

EPILOGUE

The birth of man is an unending mystery. It is the journey within for the beyonding of being. It is a journey, again, for spiritual effulgence. Otherwise man could have been else than man.

What prompts man to be more than man ? What exalts him within the to reduce himself to a cipher ? What inspires him to re-discover himself from all possible points of view ? These and numerous other queries haunt the human mind.

Spiritually, man gains from three dimensions of consciousness, which in terms of Gandhian spiritualism may be identified as external, internal and spiral phenomena of human behaviour. While the external and the internal spiritual phenomena are manifested in practice of perfection, the spiral phenomena of spiritualism are continually evolved in course of spiritual actions.

Significantly enough, Gandhi makes a comprehensive appeal to spiritual consciousness in the discovery of the ascent of man. Hence, love as a divine reflection of God in course of the activities and accomplishments of man. His concept of *daridranarayana* is one of continual spiritual efforts to identify and achieve the course of ascent in the pattern of evolution. Like Swami Vivekananda who encourages man to be effulgent like little suns in brightness of reflection in millions, Gandhi makes a unison of love and God in strengthening the multi-dimensional force of spiritual awareness to sing everywhere the glory of mankind.

Admittedly, Gandhi eyes spiritualism from the standpoint of love that represents Truth, Beauty and Goodness at the same time. Otherwise, love caged and compartmentalized loses the real spiritual aroma of identification with the All Serene. For such a spiritual vision of love, the ground is to be well furnished. The hows and whys of love as a spiritual entity in man cannot be ignored for an indefinite period. The divine spirit in man will automatically be restless. Can anyone remain indifferent to spiritual beckonings ? Can Truth as the intrinsic force of spiritualism remain dormant for ever ? As Gandhi believes and actualizes in actions, it cannot. The all-strength, all-beauty, all-knowledge of Truth haunt man all the while to merge in the beauty of the All Beautiful, All Strong or Almighty, All Knower. Hence, the genesis of spiritualism.

Gandhi, therefore, ponders over the role of education for spiritual emancipation of man in terms of individual excellence by means of prayer which is as he very significantly remarks, 'the alpha and omega of all education'. What does modern education cater for ? How far is it faithful to emancipation of spiritual excellence ? When would humanity be aware of the great contributions of man as a spiritual embodiment of God?

Realistically, man haunts for the world unknown to him. It is the world of growing mechanomania and crazy booms of romantic taboos. Is the world that cares for nobody loves everyone today? Is everyone of us a debased and arrogant Orpheus ? Is the song of humanity the song of bullets and guns ?

The destiny of man, alas, is the destiny of extinction. The riot is not elsewhere but within. The heartland of humanity frantically awaits the swansong of spiritual awakening for which Gandhi becomes a martyr to the cause of Light.

The sadness that has fallen upon global humanity awaits the poignance of perfection in listening to the Orphic voice of the martyr. Perhaps it is the same spiritual experiences that we need as Rabindranath Tagore muses:

> On the day when the lotus bloomed, alas, my mind was straying, and I knew it not. My basket was empty and the flower remained unheeded.
>
> Only now and again a sadness fell upon me, and I started up from my dream and felt a sweet trace of strange fragrance in the south wind.
>
> That vague sweetness made my heart ache with longing and it seemed to me that it was the eager breath of the summer seeking for its completion.
>
> I know not then that it was so near, that it was mine, and that this perfect sweetness had blossomed in the depth of my own heart.

— Rabindranath Tagore : *Gitanjali (Song Offerings)* Macmillan India Limited, Macmillan Pocket Tagore Edition, 1989, No. XX, p. 12.

The aching sweetness of Light in the depth of everyone's heart awaits an efflorescence in the perfection of spiritual vision and Gandhi as an ardent spiritual thinker wants humanity to be faithful to the finer feelings and nobler sentiments that from time to time contribute towards the ascent of man as an unparalleled evolutionary force.

The river of life rushes through the waves of fulfilment. The storms of life beckon the promises of poignance. Yet the waves of fulfilment and the storms of life bring forth a certain pattern of disharmony and illusion, which necessitates a look within and a look anew. Gandhi visualizes man not merely a taskmaster but also a framer of his own frame in the casket of catholicity of vision. The so-called worship of God in the form of observance of religion misses the essence of spiritualism, for *bhakti* as Gandhi always maintains, is the spirit that is mused in the melody of modesty — a waning force of spiritualism in a battered world of ours.

To spiritually visualize God as the Brother amongst brothers of mankind and enjoy sharing the experiences of happiness and sufferings of humanity are the vibrant lessons of poignance that must not, as Gandhi warns again and again, be ignored. Apathy and ostracism have already stood in the way of spiritual excellence. Should man ignore man and orphanize the *Narayana* who symbolizes the highest embodiment of the All Serene?

Spiritualism — the right road to become what we should be — is the only way to encounter the inner 'I' in order to endear and adorn the best 'We'. The cathedral of inner consciousness, the Holy Grail of the *Vaishnava,* stands calm and sombre in the exquisite grandeur of a giant with specs and a wand and piece of loin cloth proclaiming the victory of man as a great spiritual force.

Do we visualize the ever-efflorescent loving loin-clothed *fakir* spiritualizing the Light Eternal?

BIBLIOGRAPHY

Aurobindo, Sri : *The Ideal of Human Unity*, Sri Aurobindo Pathamandir, Calcutta, 1972.

—— : *The Human Cycle*, Sri Aurobindo Pathamandir, Calcutta, 1972.

—— : *The Life Divine*, Sri Aurobindo Ashram, Pondicherry.

Bhattacharya, Buddhadeva : *Evolution of the Political Philosophy of Gandhi*, Calcutta Book House, Calcutta, 1969.

Chakrabarti, Mohit : *Gandhian Mysticism*, Atlantic Publishers & Distributors, New Delhi, 1989.

—— : *The Gandhian Dimensions of Education*, Daya Publishing House, Delhi, 1990.

—— : *Gandhian Aesthetics*, Atlantic Publishers & Distributors, New Delhi, 1990.

—— : *Gandhian Humanism*, Concept Publishing Company, New Delhi, 1992.

Desai, Valji Govindji (Ed.) : *The Diary of Mahadev Desai*, Navajivan Publishing House, Ahmedabad, 1953.

Diwakar, R.R. : *Gandhi, the Spiritual Soeker*, Bharatiya Vidya Bhavan, Bombay.

Gandhi, M.K. : *An Autobiography*.

—— : *Hind Swaraj or Indian Home Rule*.

—— : *From Yeravda Mandir*.

—— : *Harijan*.

—— : *Young India*.

—— : *In Search of the Supreme*.

—— : *Speeches and Writings of Mahatma Gandhi*.

Mahadevan, T.K. (Ed.) : *Truth and Non-violence*, Gandhi Peace Foundation, New Delhi, 1970.

Nehru, Jawaharlal : *Mahatma Gandhi*, Asia Publishing House, Bombay, 1949.

Prabhu, R.K. & Rao, U.R. (Compiled) : *The Mind of Mahatma Gandhi*, Oxford University Press, London, 1945.

Pyarelal : *Mahatma Gandhi : The Last Phase*, Navajivan Publishing House, Ahmedabad. 1958.

——: *The Epic Fast*, Mohanlal Maganlal Bhatt, Ahmedabad.

Ranganathananda, Swami : *Eternal Values for a Changing Society*, Bharatiya Vidya Bhavan, Bombay, Vol. I., 1984.

Rao, V.K.R.V. : *The Gandhian Alternative to Western Socialism*, Bharatiya Vidya Bhavan, Bombay, 1981.

Radhakrishnan, S. : *Occasional Speeches and Writings*, Publications Division, Government of India, Third Series, 1963.

Spratt, P. : *Gandhism : An Analysis*, Huxley Press, Madras.

Tendulkar, D.G. : *Mahatma*, (Vols I-VIII), Publications Division, Government of India.

Vivekananda Swami : *The Complete Works of Swami Vivekananda*, Advaita Ashrama, Calcutta, 1982.

The Visva-Bharati Quarterly, Visva-Bharati, Gandhi Number (Vols I-VIII), Santiniketan, 1970.

Tagore, Rabindranath : *Song Offerings : (Gitanjali)*, Macmillan India Ltd. New Delhi, 1983.

Wolfenstein, Victor : *The Revolutionary Personality : Lenin, Trotsky, Gandhi*, Princeton University Press, New Jersey, 1967.

INDEX

Abhaya, 61
Abstraction, 100
Adhibhuta, 73, 74
Adhiyajna, 74
Adhyatma, 74
Advaita, 22, 89
Ahimsa, 15, 16, 58, 61, 62, 86, 91, 105, 117, 139
All Beautiful, 100, 109, 116, 118, 125, 130, 151, 163, 169, 178
All Glorious, 161
All Joyful, 68, 69
Allah, 142
Amrita, 104
Ananda, 55
Animal passions, 37
Aparigraha (non-possession), 133
Arambha, 151
Atmajnam, 163
Atman, 65
Atmanubhuti, 163
Aurobindo, 73, 75, 76, 113, 118, 122
Basava, 171
Basic education, 38, 53
Bhagavata, 18
Bhagvadgita, 108
Bhakta, 156
Bhakti, 148, 149, 150, 152, 179
Bhakti-yoga, 159
Bhattacharya, Buddhadeva, 45
Bible, 18, 147
Boer war, 14
Brahma, 65, 73
Brahmacharya, 19, 40, 49, 64, 65, 66, 158
Brahman, 151
Brahmin, 124
Buddha, 110
Buddhi, 78
Buddhist, 138
Chaitanya, 144
Chakravarti, S., 60
Chapati, 92
Charkha, 52, 174
Chhilam (earthen pipe), 153
Christian, 18, 138
Corporal punishment, 27-28
Corruption, 36
Criticism, 45, 114
Crystallization, 98
Dana, 135
Daridranarayana, 50, 133, 177
Das Gupta, Sugata, 51
Dayananda, 143, 144
Desai, Valji Govindji, 58
Dhyana yoga, 87
Diverse programmes, 52
Discipline, 75
Discovery of errors, 86
Dissemination, global mankind for, 16
Divine being, 99
Divine law, 90
Diwakar, R.R., 163, 166
Education, 26, 30, 32, 43, 52
    conference, 41
    slavish pattern of, 43
    true economics of, 33
Efflorescence, 69, 105, 136
Ekatvatva, 162
Erudition, 24
European war, 14
Evolution, 19
Exhibitionism, 19
Exploitation, 60
Fakir, 52
Fanaticism, 18, 101
Fasting, 19
Freedom-struggle, 50
Gandhi, M.K., 11, 12, 15, 17, 18, 21, 23, 26, 34, 40, 47, 49, 52, 54, 58, 62, 65, 70, 72, 74, 77, 82, 85, 88, 92, 97, 108, 115, 125, 140, 144, 150, 165, 174
    conception, 59
    elucidates, 31, 34
    explicit exposition, 49
    eye spiritualism, 177
    independence day message, 51
    own experience, 27
    own interpretation, 68
    own spiritual mission, 148
    programmes, 55
    sarvodaya, 59
    social revolution, 50
Gandhian spiritualism, 13, 22, 32, 54, 57, 64, 112, 113, 163, 169, 177
    aesthetics of, 80, 83

strategies, 34
Gift of life, 117
Gita, 49, 63, 67, 73, 84, 87, 103, 108, 124, 150, 160
Glorification, 72
Gnostic energy, 163
God-realization, 163
Great white Thorne, 41
Gunas, 109
Gymnasium, 161
Harijans, 37
Harmony, 11, 18
Himalayan cave, 21
Hindu, 138
philosophy, 139
Intellectual training, 32
Intense mental struggle, 125
Jesus, 110
Jnana-yoga, 141, 159
Kabir, 144, 171
Kalema, 139
Karma, 152
Karuna, 25
Kathiawad, 19
Khadi, 37
department, 151
movement, 89
Khuda, 142
Khudai Raj, 78
Kriplani, J.B., 82, 83, 84
Kurukshetra, 33
Language, 16, 29, 112
Law of Love, 90
Lingayats, 171
Living force, 109
law, 97
Mahatmaship, 49
Mammoth meeting, 101
Manifestation, 23, 41, 53, 55
Manomayah, 65
Mantras, 31
Mascare, J., 173
Materialism, 100
Maya, 160
Miseducation, 56
Modern world, 169
Moral training, 30
Muhammad, 110
Mundaka Upanishad, 65
Mushrooms, 11
Muslim, 138
Mysticism, 114
Naitalim, 103
Nanak, 144
Narayana, 179
Nehru, Jawaharlal, 169
New education, 137
New testament, 108
Non-violence, 46, 115
spirit of, 15
Numerous, 100
Nyaya, 61
Occupation, 32, 41
Omnipresent, 125
Over-confidence, 86
Pad, 159
Panchama, 70
Parathabhavana, 107
Par excellence, 13, 123
Pari passu, 34
Patanjali's yoga sutras, 132
Perumal, Alasinga, 140
Polak, H.S., 15
Political education, 15-16
emancipation, 45
Prabhu, R.K., 13, 14, 37, 40, 46, 63, 75, 98, 99, 116, 142, 147, 163, 175
Practical religion, 42
Prana, 74
Primary education, 41, 44
Pupils discrimination, 31
Puratan, 83
Purification, 137
Pyarelal, 39, 43, 76, 100, 114
Radhakrishnan, S., 33
Raja yoga, 132
Ramakrishna Paramahamsa, 143, 144
Ramananda, 171
Ramanama, 76, 77
Ramanuja, 170
Rama Raj, 37, 53, 77
Ramatirth, 143
Ramdas, 144
Rammohan Roy, 144
Rao, U.R., 13, 14, 37, 40, 46, 63, 75, 98, 99, 147
Rao, V.K.R.V., 106, 107
Redcross work, 14
Religion, 17, 54
efflorescence, 105
Restraints, 14
Restriction, 19
Revolution, 120
Revolutionary's heroism, 121
Rishis, 31
Rolland, Romain, 13
Romulo, Carlos, 171, 172
Rose of God, 119
Ruskin, 60
Sadhana, 153
Samabhavana (equability), 133
Sanatan, 83

Sankara, 170
Sans, 123, 126, 174
Sannyasa (renunciation), 29
Sarvamangala-bhavana, 76
Sarvodaya, 57, 59, 60, 61, 62, 66, 69, 71, 76, 78, 106, 174
Sastras, 84
Sattva, 84
Satyagraha, 12, 19, 60, 91, 118
Satyagrahi, 45, 70
Satyameva Jayate, 61
Satyanarayana, 62, 80, 92, 121
Second World War, 159
Self-assessment, 41
Self-confidence, 173
Self-deception, 71
Self-development, 54
Self-purification, 11, 12, 16, 47, 103, 113, 121, 173
Self-realization, 19, 28, 29, 31, 54, 74, 81, 116, 158, 163
Self-restraint, 19, 20, 21, 44
Self-sacrifice, 224
Self-satisfaction, 24, 58
Self-surrender, 121
Self-understanding, 41
Sentimentalism, 17
Separatism, 101
Sex complex, 36
Sexual passion, 35
Shukla, Chandrasekhar, 15
Sikhs, 138, 171
Social harmonization, 50
Socialism, 48
South Africa, 19
Spirit eternal, 25, 72, 145, 174
Spiritual athletes, 124
 attainment, 30
 consciousness, 66, 130
 education, 26, 28, 41, 55
  development, 27
  manifestation, 36
 efflorescence, 69
 emancipation, 142, 156, 178
 experience, 34
 poverty, 59
 training, 28
Spiritualism, 11, 23, 57, 95
 aesthetic component of, 89, 91, 95
 apostle eternal, 95
 ascent for, 12
 components of, 14, 17, 81
 dynamic force of, 72
 embodiment of, 57
 emergence of, 53
 essence of, 17
 exponent of, 37
 finer visions of, 19
 manifestation of, 53
 message of, 78
 objective of, 21
 poignance of, 166
 pursuit of, 81
 significance of, 399
 teaching of, 46
 true essence of, 18
Spratt, P., 114
St. Mathew, 71
Sthitadhi, 80, 88
Strategic components, 60
 force, 61
Strategies, 19
Suddhi, 134
Supreme Spiritual Power, 163
Swami Shradhhanandaji, 123
Swami Vivekananda, 130, 131, 134, 140, 141, 143, 144, 148, 149, 152, 157, 160, 162, 163, 165, 167, 177
Swaraj, 37, 103
Synchronization, 58, 154
Tabligh, 134
Tagore, Devendranath, 144
Tagore, Rabindranath, 69, 79, 123, 124, 126, 174, 178
Takli, 42
Tamas, 109
Tapas meditation, 130-31
Tapasya, 24, 54
Tenatyaktena bhunjithah, 63, 64
Tendulkar, D.G., 36, 38, 41, 44, 101, 103, 110, 112, 120, 124, 133, 137, 138, 148, 159
Terrible calamity, 101
Tolstoy Farm, 26, 29, 41
Truth, efflorescence of, 16
 full vision of, 17, 105
Tukaram, 144
Tulsidas, 144
Tyagi (detached), 140
Upanishads, 64
Upasak, 103
Utilitarianism, 11, 43, 52, 55, 171
Universal Dawn, 59
Vaishnava, 159, 179
Vidyarthi, 40
Violation, 14, 118
Wisdom-yoga, 158
Yoga, 78
Yogi, 66, 67, 135, 145
Young India, 13
Zulu Rebellion, 14